SOUTH YORKSHIRE COUNTY ARCHAEOLOGY MONOGI

SAXON CHURCHES IN SOUTH YORKSHIRE

by

P. F. RYDER, B.A., M. Phil.

SOUTH YORKSHIRE COUNTY ARCHAEOLOGY SERVICE

WITH A CONTRIBUTION BY:

DAVID HEY, M.A., Ph.D.,

Preface

Anglo-Saxon churches, the oldest buildings to survive in the English countryside, have always held a special fascination for the archaeologist and historian, amateur and professional alike. This monograph looks at the oldest churches in South Yorkshire, and includes in-depth investigations of the building histories and important features of seven of the most interesting. These include the 8th century minster church at Conisbrough and the puzzling 11th century buildings at Brodsworth and Hooton Pagnell, which in style are hybrids between the Saxon and Norman traditions. Surviving sculptural fragments of the same era are described and illustrated. During the compilation of South Yorkshire County Council's Ancient Monuments and Sites Record, from which much of the information in these pages is taken, what is probably the earliest piece of Christian sculpture in the county was discovered built into a wall of the church at Darfield. Later carvings show the same overlap between Saxon and Norman traditions as is seen in some church buildings.

Also included is a gazetteer of all the medieval churches in South Yorkshire, with notes on the date of the buildings and features of especial interest.

This monograph can be used as a form of guide book to the seven churches described in detail. The reader should however bear in mind that the prime purpose of a parish church is certainly not to be a museum or ancient monument. Nevertheless most churches do welcome visitors, although nowadays few are left open. Arrangements to inspect the buildings should be made with the incumbent or churchwarden, whose telephone numbers are listed in the Diocesan Directory under the name of the church.

If the writing of this monograph leads to a great understanding and sympathy for the ancient churches of South Yorkshire then its purpose will have been well served. We owe it to future generations to see that these buildings are preserved.

Acknowledgements

In preparing this monograph I have received considerable assistance and kindness from many quarters which I gratefully acknowledge.

The fieldwork which made this monograph possible was carried out only through the goodwill and co-operation of the incumbents of the County's ancient parish churches. In particular the Rev. I. Chisholm of Conisbrough cheerfully tolerated considerable inconvenience whilst measured sections of his church's nave walls were being prepared.

The chapter on pre-Conquest and Overlap sculpture was prepared with the assistance of Mr. J. T. Lang, Archaeological Consultant to the Diocese of Durham.

I am also indebted to a number of other friends and fellow workers who have contributed information and assistance; Mr. S. Coleman for assistance with fieldwork at Brodsworth and Conisbrough; Mr. G. Davies who first recognised the importance of the pre-Conquest fabric at Conisbrough; Dr. D. Hey of the University of Sheffield who contributed the chapter on the historical background to South Yorkshire's Saxon Churches and whose enthusiasm and advice have been invaluable; Mr. S. R. Jones of Sheffield City Polytechnic and Mr. R. Morris of the University of Leeds with whom I have had many useful discussions.

My thanks are also due to a number of my colleagues in the Department of Recreation, Culture and Health, namely Mr. F. St. D. Rowntree, Mrs. C. M. Short and Mr. J. H. Little for their encouragement as well as professional and editorial advice and assistance; also to Mr. F. Saunders for providing reconstructed perspective impressions of a number of the churches described, as well as the cover design and illustrations.

Finally I would like to express my appreciation to Mrs. P. Marshall who typed the final text with great patience, expertise and good humour.

P.F.R. 1982

Contents

The Study of Old Churches

In almost every English town and village the parish church is the oldest surviving building, usually standing on a site which has been continuously in use for meeting and worship since the first coming of Christianity to the area, and which may have done duty as a religious site in even earlier periods. A great many church fabrics show work dating back to the Norman period, with evidence of a gradual enlargement throughout the following centuries.

Tracing the building history of an old church, 'reading the fabric' as it were, is one of the problems (or pleasures) of the archaeologist, amateur or professional. The popular concept of archaeology being confined to the digging of holes in the ground is quite false, each wall of an old church is in effect an archaeological section exposed for all to see. Its interpretation may be simple and straightforward, or may cause academic controversy for generations. In South Yorkshire, look at the south wall of the chancel at Laughton-en-le-Morthen for such an example of vertical archaeology. Is the red sandstone of the lower courses Anglo-Saxon masonry *in situ* or simply re-used stone? What was the form of the Norman windows of which only fragments survive? Are the present windows all work of the same remodelling scheme in the late 14th century? Many of the problems are not easy to resolve conclusively.

In South Yorkshire, medieval fabric survives in 71 old churches. In 50 of these, parts are of 12th century or earlier date. It is with the earlier churches that this monograph is primarily concerned. A handful of partly Anglo-Saxon churches have been known for some time, Burghwallis, Conisbrough and Laughton, but others with pre-Norman features have not previously been described in detail. This investigation is not simply concerned with churches that can be dated categorically to before 1066, the year of the Norman invasion. The pre-Norman styles and motifs were only gradually displaced, at any rate in the case of village churches. Thus we have the concept of the 'Saxo-Norman Overlap', a hybrid style between the clearly recognisable Saxon and the equally distinctively Norman. An Overlap style in church sculpture (crosses, grave stones and fonts) has been recognised in the South Yorkshire area, and a corresponding class of architecture might only be expected.

The typical development of an English parish church through the centuries might best be cited by considering a theoretical example. A timber Saxon church might be replaced in the 11th century by a stone building consisting of an aisleless nave and chancel. In the later 12th century enlargement might be effected by the addition of a west tower and aisles to the nave, the masonry of the original nave walls being preserved at the corners and above the inserted Norman arches of the arcades. In the 13th century the original chancel might be rebuilt on a larger scale with typical Early English lancet windows, and in the 15th century the church re-windowed in the Perpendicular style, a chantry chapel built onto the north side of the chancel and a south porch added. The turbulence of the Reformation in the mid 16th century, and of the Civil War in the 17th, were not conducive to church building, and the building remained little altered except for repairs and the replacement of a few windows.

In the 19th century most old churches suffered a restoration, with the Victorian revival of enthusiasm for Gothic architecture. In some cases this was carried out well, only the worst of the post-medieval alterations being replaced by work in a more suitably Gothic style. Often however a less sensitive treatment befell the building, with genuine medieval features being torn out to be replaced by Victorian Gothic extravagance. The more savage restorations caused an outcry at the time; a pamphlet published in Sheffield detailing some local restorations is dedicated to 'Northern Vandals' in general and five architects in particular.

In some cases the restorers have confused the evidence as regards the interpretation of the building's history. Blocked openings and straight joints, the evidence of the piecemeal medieval enlargement and alteration of the church, were erased when walls were re-faced, and original sculpture and mouldings re-tooled so that today it may be difficult to distinguish a genuine medieval feature from one that is wholly Victorian.

Examinations and descriptions of the architecture and fabric of old churches can be classed into three groups. The first, which can only be termed superficial, can be seen in many church guide books and such publications as Pevsner's *THE BUILDINGS OF ENGLAND*. Here a wall might be dated simply by the style of the windows it contains (despite the fact that they may be later medieval insertions or even Victorian innovations) and minor features, such as joints and breaks between different masonry types, often ignored.

A second level of investigation is that in which the fabric is examined more thoroughly, inside and out, and the subtle as well as the obvious features taken into account. Changes in alignment of walls, and variations in their thickness, can be obtained from an accurate ground plan. This often reveals the development of the church to be more complex than the superficial inspection might suggest; in practise it might reveal a number of features difficult to explain, and result in more problems than answers. Documentary references, for example faculties for restorations, should also be taken into account, to sort out exactly what happened to the building in the 19th century.

The third level, at which it is hoped most structural problems will be resolved, is the full archaeological investigation, above and below ground. Obviously this can be carried out only on rare occasions, in churches which are either no longer in use, or undergoing major structural works. The half dozen structural phases identified in a 'level two' inspection might now become a dozen (as was found at Wharram Percy in North Yorkshire) with remains of Saxon timber churches coming to light beneath later floors, and evidence of unsuspected medieval alterations being uncovered. Relatively few churches have been investigated in this way. However, smaller scale works, such as the construction of a drainage trench round the building or the stripping of plaster from an internal wall, may reveal vital evidence of the building's history.

A great number of old churches have never received anything more than a relatively superficial examination, especially in areas such as South Yorkshire where there is no long-established archaeological society with a bent towards ecclesiology. The study of church fabrics was a popular pastime of the 19th century antiquary, but his modern archaeologist counterpart has tended to concentrate on other things. It is probably true to say that church buildings have been relatively neglected over the last half century, with the exception of areas in which the Royal Commission on Historical Monuments have worked. With the excavation of churches such as Wharram Percy and Deerhurst (in Gloucestershire) interest in ecclesiology has reawakened.

What this monograph attempts is a 'level two' examination and interpretation of seven South Yorkshire churches, concentrating on their pre-Conquest and Overlap phases, but not ignoring their later development, or their monuments and fittings, where these are of interest, so that the interested laymay may use it as a kind of guidebook to these churches. A number of other churches in the county, where there is slighter evidence of early fabric or sculpture, are described more briefly.

An Introduction to Anglo-Saxon Architecture

Anglo-Saxon architecture does not have a single easily definable style in the manner of the architecture of the later medieval period. In the 14th or 15th century an easily recognizable type of window tracery may be datable to within 50 years, or even less, whichever part of the country one is in. Not so before the Norman Conquest. What survives is fabric and architectural features in between 400 and 500 churches, ranging in date from c.600 to c.1100, and encompassing a wide range of localised types and styles. Virtually all these buildings are small parish churches. A more unified style of architecture might have appeared in the minsters and great abbey churches, but almost all of these were swept away by the rebuilding zeal of the Norman conquerors. Wulfstan of Worcester, according to William of Malmesbury, lamented at the time "wretches that we are, we destroy the work of our saintly forebears, because we think in our pride that we can do better".

From this scatter of pre-Conquest parish churches, preserving a wide variety of fabric types and architectural features, archaeologists and historians have laboured to construct typologies and discern means of dating. The fact that pre-Norman buildings survived in this country and possessed certain distinctive characteristics was recognised only in 1817 by Thomas Rickman, who listed churches which he considered to be of Saxon date. By 1925 Professor Baldwin Brown had extended this list to over 200, and dated many of these to one of three periods within the Saxon era, designated by him simply as A (600-800), B (800-950, the time of the Viking raids) and C (950-1100).

In recent years our knowledge of Anglo-Saxon churches has been increased by a number of important excavations, and detailed examinations of the fabric of several churches. Such research has meant that the previously accepted dates for some of the better known Saxon churches have had to be revised. Dr. H. M. Taylor and Joan Taylor, whose major three volume *ANGLO SAXON ARCHITECTURE* is currently the definitive work on the subject, conclude that "the time is not ripe for firm pronouncements about the dates of more than a handful of the buildings ...".

The use of the year 1100 as the terminal date for Saxon architecture may be puzzling. Whilst the Anglo-Saxon period came to an end politically in 1066 with William's invasion, the Anglo-Saxon style certainly continued in use for quite a number of years, especially in the more rural areas. In some parts of the country (South Yorkshire is one of them) the incoming of the new Norman style was gradual, and churches continued to be built with some Anglo-Saxon features well into the 12th century. The recognition of this fact has led to the concept of the 'Saxo-Norman Overlap', to which a considerable number of churches can now be ascribed. Overlap churches are not necessarily of post-Conquest date. There is evidence that Edward the Confessor imported continental masons in the decade prior to 1066 to erect the great churches, Waltham Abbey and Westminster Abbey, in the Norman style although technically speaking they are of Anglo-Saxon date. However, in the village churches the use together of Saxon and Norman features generally points to a date in the half century or so after the Norman Conquest.

In the following brief survey of the distinctive features now held to be typical of Anglo-Saxon work, special attention is given to those found in churches in the North of England, i.e. Yorkshire and further north, and to distinguishing characteristics between Anglo-Saxon and Norman work. The writer is greatly indebted to Dr. H. M. and Joan Taylor's magnum opus.

CHURCH PLANS

The majority of Anglo-Saxon churches have seen so much alteration and enlargement that their original plan is difficult to determine. The most common plan amongst the smaller churches appears to be a simple rectangular nave and chancel, quite often with a western tower, very much the same plan as many small Norman churches.

Few Saxon churches, and none in the North of England, were aisled in the common medieval sense. However, many show evidence of having had chambers or ranges of chambers on one or both sides of the main body of the building. These distinctively pre-Conquest chambers are termed porticus, and tended to be quite separate from the body of the church. They were entered through a relatively narrow doorway, unlike the transepts or side chapels of the later medieval churches which opened into the nave or chancel by a wide arch. Insufficient is known of pre-Conquest church ritual to be sure of the use of the porticus; they may have been side chapels for prayer and meditation, or perhaps reserved for burials. Where there is a single porticus it is tempting to see it as an equivalent to the later vestry.

Belfry towers, usually at the west end of the nave, are generally thought to be of late Saxon date (i.e. 10th or 11th century). There is evidence that some (as at Ledsham in West Yorkshire or Monkwearmouth in Tyne and Wear) are built on top of earlier western porches.

A feature which appears to have been commonplace in Saxon churches is the western gallery, or high level chamber, above the nave. The only evidence of this which commonly survives is a high level doorway, now usually blocked, in the east wall of the tower.

A distinct 'Northumbrian' group of Saxon churches has been recognised, to which Conisbrough in South Yorkshire almost certainly belongs. The characteristics of these are naves which are relatively long and narrow, with high side walls, and much narrower and shorter chancels. The latter, however, rarely survive.

WALL FABRIC

Anglo-Saxon builders tended towards one of two very different types of wall construction, either the use of megalithic walling using very large stones where such were available, or simple rubble fabric (usually with substantial angle quoins). Coursed ashlar work is almost invariably evidence of Norman or later workmanship.

Herringbone fabric, in which alternating courses of rubble or small flat stones are laid diagonally to produce an attractive pattern, provides a means of producing courses of regular height from stones of varying thickness. The date of herringbone work has occasioned much controversy in the past; it is now generally accepted as having been in use both before and after the Norman Conquest (see the description of Burghwallis Church below). In Yorkshire churches the use of herringbone fabric, or even just the occasional course of stones laid diagonally, is usually taken as an indicator of Saxo-Norman Overlap, or at any rate Early Norman work.

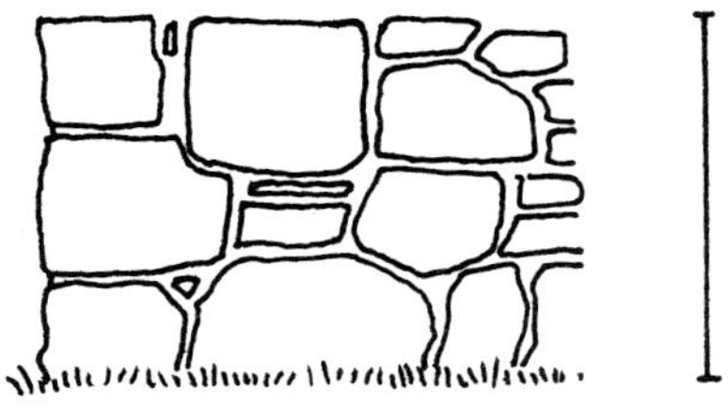

1 metre

Megalithic walling - using large blocks

1 metre

Rubble wall, uncoursed, with side-alternate quoins

1 metre

Herringbone fabric, with side-alternate quoins

Anglo-Saxon builders seem to have happily utilised material from earlier buildings where this was available. The ruins of Roman buildings in the City of York, conveniently sited for the transport of stone by river, provided material for the construction of several Saxon churches. The little church at Escomb in Durham, the least altered pre-Conquest building in the North of England, appears to have been constructed of stone from the nearby fort of Vinovia (Binchester) as the Roman diagonal tooling of much of its masonry testifies. The chancel arch itself is thought to have been removed bodily from a Roman building, and a similar origin has been put forward for the tower arch at Corbridge in Northumberland.

WALL THICKNESS

A general rule is that Anglo-Saxon walls tend to be thinner than Norman. The Saxon builders seem to have placed considerable confidence in the strength of their mortar and after a thousand years this can be seen to have been quite justified. Taylor quotes the average wall thickness for 186 English Saxon naves as being 2 ft. 7 ins. (0.78m.), whereas Norman nave walls are usually over 3 ft. (0.91m.) thick.

ANGLE QUOINS

The use of distinctive angle quoins is one of the best known features of Anglo-Saxon work, one recognised by Rickman when he first advanced his arguments for the survival of Saxon churches. Rickman described the two most common quoin types, the 'long-and-short' (his term) and what he referred to simply as 'quoined work' but which has now been classed as 'side alternate'. As discussed in the account of Bolton-on-Dearne church, these two major quoin types have distinctly regional characteristics.

Virtually all of the Northumbrian group of Saxon churches have side alternate quoins, defined by Taylor as "stones laid on their sides with the longer edges of the stones in successive courses placed alternately first along one wall and then along the other". Side alternate quoins were still in frequent use after the Conquest, but the Saxon examples almost always use larger stones. Where the quoining can be classed as megalithic (as at Burghwallis) it provides a fairly safe indication of a pre-Conquest fabric.

Long-and-short quoins, almost totally absent from Northumbria, have tall pillar stones alternating with flat clasping stones which serve to bond the quoin into the wall. They are not found in the earliest Saxon churches and are thought to be a late 9th century invention. Neither are they used after the Norman Conquest, except in very rare instances.

TOWER AND CHANCEL ARCHES

None of South Yorkshire's four undoubtedly Saxon churches retains a tower or chancel arch. Where these survive elsewhere, in the smaller churches, they generally tend to be simple round-headed openings of a single square order, often relatively tall and narrow. Occasionally a more elaborate example occurs, as in the tower arch at Carlton-in-Lindrick just across the Nottinghamshire border, with its moulded arch and jamb shafts with decorated capitals.

The use of through stones, spanning the whole thickness of the wall, in such arches is a good indication of Saxon date. Nevertheless there are a considerable number of simple round-headed tower and chancel arches which do not use this technique. It is difficult to place these on one side or the other of the Norman Conquest. The chancel arch at Hooton Pagnell is a case in point.

DOORWAYS

Several types of Saxon doorway have survived, mostly quite easily distinguished from Norman work. Their jambs are generally cut straight through the wall without any rebate at all, the actual door probably being hung on the inside wall face. Norman doors are almost always rebated for a door hung between the centre and outer face of the wall. The south door at Burghwallis is unusual in that it has a rebate only 6½ ins. (0.16m.) from the inside wall face.

The through-stone technique often seen in Saxon tower and chancel arches is also frequently used in door jambs of the period, the size of stone used in the jamb generally being much greater than that in the adjacent walling. The jamb stones may be laid in what Baldwin Brown termed 'Escomb fashion', alternately upright and flat, a technique which may have inspired the development of long-and-short angle quoins.

Most pre-Conquest door heads are semicircular, a simple square order of voussoirs being the most usual form. A band of stripwork (usually of square section) which encloses the head of the arch in the manner of the medieval hoodmould but is continued down the jambs as well is a characteristic feature. It is this that distinguishes the south door at Finningley as Anglo-Saxon in style, even though it may be post-Conquest in actual date (see Gazetteer of South

Yorkshire Churches). Stripwork also outlines the north door at Laughton-en-le-Morthen, and a trace of it survives on the east jamb of the porticus arch at Bolton-on-Dearne.
Architectural textbooks often illustrate doorways with gabled (i.e. triangular) heads as characteristic Anglo-Saxon work, but these are really quite rare. Where they do occur it is usually as high level doorways in towers. The ruins of the monastic buildings at Jarrow, datable to the 1070's and very much in the Overlap style include a good gabled doorway in the wall on the west side of the cloister garth.
Other pre-Conquest doors have simple flat lintels, for example the north door at Escomb, or an arch, either semicircular or segmental, cut in the underside of a monolithic slab, as in the north and south doors of the former west porch, later raised into a tower, at Bardsey on the outskirts of Leeds.

WINDOWS

Two distinct types of Anglo-Saxon window are recognised, the single-splayed window (where the narrowest part of the opening is on the line of the outer wall face and the splay totally internal) and the double-splayed (where the narrowest part of the aperture is in the centre of the wall, splayed out both internally and externally). Single-splayed windows occur in Saxon churches in most parts of the country, but double-splayed are concentrated in the South of England and East Anglia, one of the reasons for this being the type of building material available. Taylor suggests that the double-splayed form of window was easier to construct when rubble rather than good building stone had to be used in wall construction. In the Northern counties, where good stone was often to hand, double-splayed windows are rare, and the single-splayed ones are generally of monolithic construction, with their heads cut from a single slab. Whereas double-splayed windows appear only in Late Saxon churches (Baldwin Brown's period C), and are not used by Norman builders, single-splayed forms continued in use from the earliest Saxon into the medieval period. Several Northumbrian churches possess examples which it is difficult to date to one side of the Conquest or the other.
It is now often difficult to determine whether an early window was glazed, closed with some other material or simply left open. Double-splayed windows often appear to have been provided with mid-wall slabs of stone or wood (examples of both survive) which might have carried glass, horn or linen. Several recent excavations have yielded fragments of Anglo-Saxon coloured glass, the occurrence of which at Escomb suggests that it was in use at even the smaller churches. Two of the chancel windows at Jarrow are closed by thin stone slabs pierced by smaller openings, one circular and one round-headed. It has been realised for some time that the function of these was to carry glass, and one has recently been re-glazed with Anglo-Saxon coloured glass found during the excavation of the adjacent monastic complex.
In shape most Saxon windows are round-headed openings, relatively small and often set quite high in the wall. Square-headed windows occur at a number of churches, for example in the north nave wall at Escomb. An interesting group of circular windows is mostly restricted to the South and East, most examples being double-splayed. The two examples at Burghwallis are unusual, but neither is in situ so the original form of their openings is unknown. A few examples of gable-headed windows also occur. The well-known example at Deerhurst is often illustrated, but there are none in the North of England.

BELFRY OPENINGS

The use of double belfry openings in which a mid-wall shaft supports a through-stone slab was one of the features that Rickman originally cited as characteristic of pre-Conquest buildings. Such a double or two-light opening is certainly the most common form in the upper stages of Anglo-Saxon towers, although single openings do occur as well (for instance on the east side of the tower at Bardsey, which has conventional double openings in the other three walls). In some cases, the twin openings are enclosed under a semicircular arch of stripwork, as in six of the churches of the Northumbrian group. Three of these, Billingham, Bywell and Ovingham, have an additional circular sound hole cut through the tympanum above the main openings and beneath the stripwork arch. The heads of the main openings are usually of monolithic construction.

Pre-Conquest belfry openings
(top stage of tower later medieval)
Monk Fryston

Norman belfry openings
Campsall

The common form of Norman two-light belfry opening is quite different in construction from the Saxon type, having a mid-wall shaft supporting a tympanum considerably thinner than the wall itself, and recessed from both inner and outer wall faces, being enclosed under an arch proper rather than an outline of stripwork. However, the overlap of Saxon and Norman styles is typified in quite a number of double belfry openings. At Hornby in North Yorkshire the belfry openings are of typical Saxon form, except that the jambs are of well dressed masonry and the mid-wall shafts have cushion capitals hinting at the Norman style. The Burghwallis belfry openings, although still reminiscent of pre-Conquest work in overall form (two lights without any enclosing arch) are one stage further away from it, the through-stone being carried by twin shafts and the individual lights having pointed rather than semicircular heads.

DECORATION AND ORNAMENT IN SAXON CHURCHES

In respect of the amount of ornament used around arches and window openings pre-Conquest churches are often plain almost to the point of severity when compared with Norman buildings. The use of the distinctive Norman ornaments, zig-zag, billet moulding, beak heads and the like, is almost invariably sure proof of post-Conquest date. The only exceptions are in one or two large churches constructed by imported Norman masons a few years before the Conquest.

The sculpture that does occur in pre-Conquest fabrics is usually of a recognisable pre-Conquest form, and often gives a useful aid to dating the building. The vine scroll and interlace on the surviving impost block of the south door at Kirby Hill, near Boroughbridge (North Yorkshire) have been dated by Collingwood to the late 9th century. However, there is some question as to whether the block may be re-used in a later Saxon fabric. At Hackness, also in North Yorkshire, the north impost of the chancel arch bears an 8th century design of interlaced dragons.

String courses in Anglo-Saxon churches seem to have served both decorative and functional purposes. A few examples carry rich carving, for example at Monkwearmouth, now almost obliterated by weathering. The functional purpose, especially important in the case of rubble walls, was to bond together the walling material and to throw clear rainwater running down the wall face. Pre-Conquest string courses tend to have a plain square section, whereas Norman and later builders favoured a chamfered profile (the use of a simple chamfer is rare in Anglo-Saxon workmanship, whether around openings or on other features).

Pilaster strips (vertical strips of stonework projecting slightly from the wall face) seem to have had a similar dual function. One of Rickman's first criteria of Saxon date (he used the term ribs), they are sometimes used, along with string courses and stripwork, to divide the external wall face up into a series of vertical panels. The tower of Barton-on-Humber church is the most northerly example known of the use of pilaster strips. Here they are used in dividing two tiers of panels, the lower round-headed, the upper with triangular heads. There has been considerable controversy over the origin and functional element of pilaster strips. Several of the earlier writers saw in such walls as those of the Barton-on-Humber tower a resemblance to a timber-framed building, and argued that they might be a decorative feature imitative of the elevation of an earlier type of building. More recently Taylor and others have pointed out the functional nature of such work in strengthening rubble walls (with which they are almost always associated, hence their absence from the Northern Counties) by providing a frame of worked stone. Evidence of this can be seen in the few cases where a wall treated in this manner can be seen in section, and the worked stone of the pilaster strips: the external projection of which is only a matter of c. ½ in. (.01m.) may be observed to extend at least 1 ft. 1 in. (0.3 m.) into the thickness of the wall.

Escomb Church, County Durham
A small 'Northumbrian' church with side alternate angle quoins and small single-splayed windows. The weathering of the roof of a former western porticus can be seen on the west gable of the nave.

St Peter's Church,
Barton upon Humber,
South Humberside.

A late Saxon tower in the southern tradition with pilaster strips forming decorative panels. The angle quoins are of long-and-short type but the faces of the 'long'stone have been cut back flush with the wall face and are concealed by plaster, giving the quoins much the same appearance as the pilaster strips.

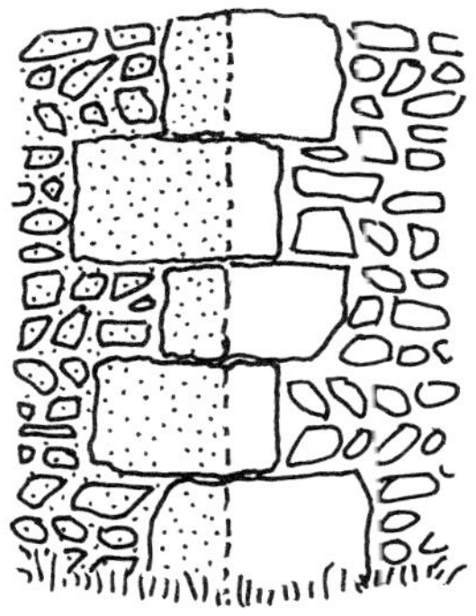

Saxon Quoin Types

Side Alternate (above)

Long-and-Short (below)

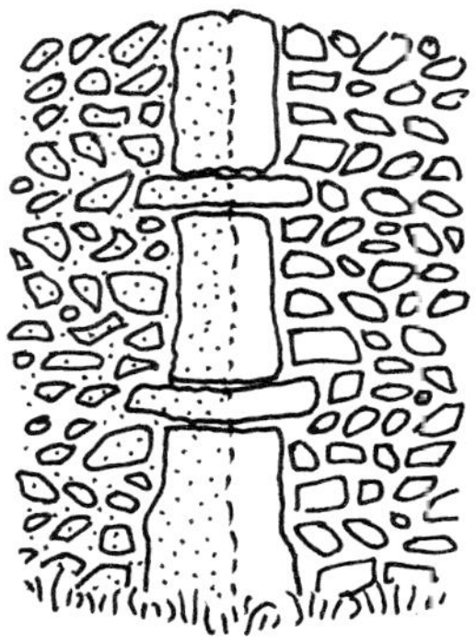

Saxon Churches in South Yorkshire: The Historical Background

The earliest references to South Yorkshire's historic churches are contained in the Domesday Book of 1086. We do not know how many had been founded by the Anglo-Saxons for no contemporary charters and only one will survive for the whole of the county. Yet it is clear from the interpretation of later evidence and from a careful examination of surviving buildings that Christianity had been established locally well before the Norman invasion. Indeed it seems likely that missionaries had gained a foothold during the time of the Romans.

One of the earliest centres was at Ecclesfield, whose name is derived from the Celtic word for a church or monastery. It is reasonable to assume that this building was still standing in the early seventh century when the Angles finally conquered the British Kingdom of Elmet. During the Middle Ages the parish of Ecclesfield covered an enormous area of some 50,000 acres, with chapels of ease at Bradfield, Chapeltown, Bolsterstone and Midhope. By 1620 (and possibly long before) Ecclesfield church was known affectionately as 'The Minster of the Moors'. It had once served the whole of Hallamshire and was the minster or mother church for south-west Yorkshire. Claims were made in 1188 that the 22,370 acres of Sheffield parish formed a chapelry dependent upon Ecclesfield, and Sheffield's former inferior status was acknowledged in 1291 and 1376.[1] Moreover, Aldward Hall, beyond Rotherham, remained a detached part of the parish of Ecclesfield until the reign of Queen Victoria.

In the north-western part of the county the medieval parish of Silkstone included Barnsley, Cawthorne, Dodworth, Hoylandswaine, Stainborough and Thurgoland, with detached portions at Cumberworth and West Bretton. The whole of the Scandinavian unit known as the wapentake of Staincross was probably originally served by a single church, for on the map the parishes of Darton, High Hoyland and Penistone fit neatly into the overall shape of Silkstone parish. The antiquity of Silkstone as the ecclesiastical centre is in some doubt, for its church is not mentioned in Domesday Book and the present building has no architectural features earlier than about 1200. Rival claims have been put forward for Cawthorne, which had a church and priest recorded in 1086, and which still has two Anglo-Saxon crosses. However, it is well known that Domesday Book did not record all the churches that were standing then, and later rebuilding may explain why Silkstone has no surviving early architecture. The matter cannot be resolved satisfactorily.

A few parishes to the north of the River Don may have been dependent upon an ecclesiastical centre beyond the present county boundary, most probably at South Kirkby whose Danish name speaks of an early church or kirk. But the majority of South Yorkshire's settlements undoubtedly owed allegiance to a minster at Conisbrough, whose substantial remains form the oldest surviving building in the county. Conisbrough was 'the king's stronghold', a name derived from Old Norse *konungr* (possibly replacing an earlier Old English *cyning*) and burh.[2] It was the centre of a royal estate on the southern border of the kingdom of Northumbria. The present county boundary is more or less the same as the Northumbrian boundary of more than a thousand years ago. Conisbrough was sited at an ancient crossing of the Don near the Strafford Sands which provided a meeting place for Yorkshire's southernmost wapentake. It was probably the chief of a series of burhs which defended the banks of the Don and the Dearne at Barnburgh, Kexbrough, Masbrough, Mexborough, Sprotborough, Stainborough and Worsbrough. Here the prehistoric and Roman Ricknield Street, which ran north along the crest of the Magnesian Limestone, was crossed by another Roman road connecting the forts at Templeborough and Doncaster. Though Roman discoveries at Conisbrough are disappointingly few, the figure now set into the east wall of the church porch is probably of Roman date. By 1086 the lordship of Conisbrough had been much reduced in size by the creation of new lordships centred on Doncaster, Laughton and Tickhill. Even so, it still included lands in twenty eight scattered settlements, mostly to the south of the Don. The castle which Hameline Plantagenet built at Conisbrough in the 1170's is the outstanding medieval monument in South Yorkshire.

Minsters were often associated with centres of royal estates, so it is entirely appropriate to find that the present church at Conisbrough incorporates a large building of an unmistakably Northumbrian style, with a dedication to St. Peter, which is normally a sign of a very early foundation. The church probably once served the whole of Conisbrough lordship, but by the time that we have firm evidence many parishes had achieved their independence. A late eleventh or early twelfth century grant from William de Warenne, lord of Conisbrough, to the priory which he founded at Lewes includes a gift of the churches and their properties at Conisbrough, Braithwell, Dinnington, Harthill, Fishlake, Hatfield (and its chapel at Thorne) and Kirk Sandall (with its chapel at Armthorpe).[3] Except for Armthorpe these churches were each associated with a manor that still belonged to the lordship of Conisbrough. They were dispersed as far as the county boundary at Harthill in the south and Thorne in the east, and their distribution strongly suggests that other places in between were once served by the mother church at Conisbrough.

South Yorkshire was a border zone, and from time to time parts of it came under the control of Mercians. The will of Wulfric Spott, a wealthy Mercian nobleman who died sometime between 1002 and 1004, shows that he had extensive possessions in northern Mercia and southern Northumbria, including the lordship of Conisbrough; parts or the whole of Doncaster, Thorpe Salvin and Wales were already detached from this lordship. The breakdown of the old estate is evident by the beginning of the eleventh century. Somehow, by 1066, Earl Edwin of Mercia had obtained a valuable and sizeable part of this estate and had built a hall or *aula* at Laughten-en-le-Morthen. The situations of Conisbrough's dependent churches at Dinnington and Harthill,and of scattered lands in the township of North Anston which remained part of Conisbrough parish, suggest that the new lordship of Laughton was carved from that of Conisbrough, but we have no evidence to say when this division took place. We can be certain, however, that Earl Edwin or some Mercian predecessor built the large pre-Conquest church at Laughton, for it was erected with long-and-short quoins in the Mercian style.

Apart from an isolated example at Whittingham in Northumberland, the only churches within the former kingdom of Northumbria which still have long-and-short quoins are at Laughton and Bolton-upon-Dearne. Bolton's place-name speaks of a former palace or mansion of indeterminate age, but by 1066 the manor had been divided between several nobles or thegns; throughout the Middle Ages Bolton was served by two rectors appointed by different lords. A church and a priest were recorded here in Domesday Book, and there is little doubt that the present nave had been built by that time. The dedication to St. Andrew is unique in South Yorkshire.

Before the Norman conquest, Earl Edwin of Mercia also held the manor of Hooton and Bilham, a few miles to the north of Laughton. Ricknield Street acted as the parish boundary for both Laughton and Hooton, and each place had a fairly large population and extensive clearings on the fertile lands that overlie the Magnesian Limestone belt. Both churches are dedicated to All Saints, a popular dedication in the later Anglo-Saxon period. Domesday Book mentions neither church nor *aula* at Hooton, but both are referred to in a grant of Ralph Pagnell's in 1089.[4] The present church does not have Mercian features but some of its architec tural details are nevertheless characteristic of the eleventh century.

It is quite feasible that some of South Yorkshire's earliest churches were built of timber. Just north of the county boundary, the Norman church at Felkirk is of sandstone, but the place-name means 'church built of planks'[5]. Local craftsmen used timber for domestic buildings throughout the Middle Ages, but surviving examples suggest that by the eleventh century stone was preferred for churches. At Hatfield, where local stone was unavailable, small boulders and pebbles were used. When Hatfield church was rebuilt in the fifteenth century Magnesian Limestone was imported from a few miles further west, but much of the Norman work was retained in the lower stages. Stone for the earliest churches was transported only short distances, but local quarries provided a variety of texture and colour. The herringbone walls at Burghwallis are arranged in a particularly attractive way and sparkle in the sun.

The Magnesian Limestone belt was the most densely settled part of the county in the Anglo-Saxon period and the early Middle Ages. Its parishes were therefore small and its churches numerous. During the later Middle Ages, however, it suffered more than most from the national decline in population. Villages such as Hooton Pagnell and Owston, which had once supported many small freeholders gradually became estate villages dominated by a squire, and at Frickley the church now stands alone in the fields for the village has gone completely. Whereas many churches in other parts of the county have been enlarged or rebuilt, a number of Magnesian Limestone churches retain much of their Anglo-Saxon or Norman structures. Burghwallis is one of these shrunken villages, and its church has never been extended with aisles or chapels. Burghwallis, Skellow and Sutton were united manorially after the Norman conquest, but the tithes of Skellow went to Owston and those of Sutton to Campsall. Burghwallis must therefore have been an independent parish before the conquest, when the manor belonged to a minor lord. The church's dedication to St. Helen also hints at an early foundation, especially as Joseph Hunter writing in 1828, refers to 'The church of St. Ellen of Burgh-Wallis'.[6] Numerous holy wells were dedicated to Elen, the Celtic goddess of armies and roads, and it may be significant that Burghwallis parish was bounded on the west by a Roman road. St. Helen ranks sixth in popularity in Yorkshire dedications because of her connections with York as the mother of Constantine, the Roman emperor who made Christianity the official religion. A dedication to either Elen or Helen is likely to have been an early one.

The two other churches that are considered in detail below also have interesting dedications. Maltby's choice of St. Bartholomew is unique in South Yorkshire, and Brodsworth's selection of St. Michael is appropriate for a hill-top site, where the saint was often depicted fighting evil in the form of a dragon. Brodsworth was another limestone parish with a Roman road as a boundary and soils that attracted early settlers, but which declined at the close of the Middle Ages. Its church and a priest are recorded in Domesday Book. The 'small and rather mean building'[7] that preceded the 1859 rebuilding at Maltby also served Hooton Levitt at the other side of the stream, and was sited in full view of the inhabitants of Hooton. The two places belonged to separate lordships after the Norman conquest and were already divided before 1066, so the parish was presumably created before our written records begin. The documentary evidence does not allow greater precision.

REFERENCES

1.	A. H. Thompson and C. T. Clay, eds.	*Fasti Parochiales*, vol. 11, 1943, pp.52-3
2.	A. H. Smith	*The Place-Names of the West Riding of Yorkshire* part 1, 1961, pp. 125-6
3.	C. T. Clay, ed.	*Early Yorkshire Charter* vol. VIII, 1949 pp. 67, 86
4.	J. Hunter	*South Yorkshire* vol. 11, 1831, p.140
5.	Smith	*op. cit.*, p. 271
6.	Hunter	*op. cit.*, vol. 11, p. 486
7.	*Ibid*	vol. 1, 264

Anglo-Saxon and 'Overlap' churches and sculpture in South Yorkshire

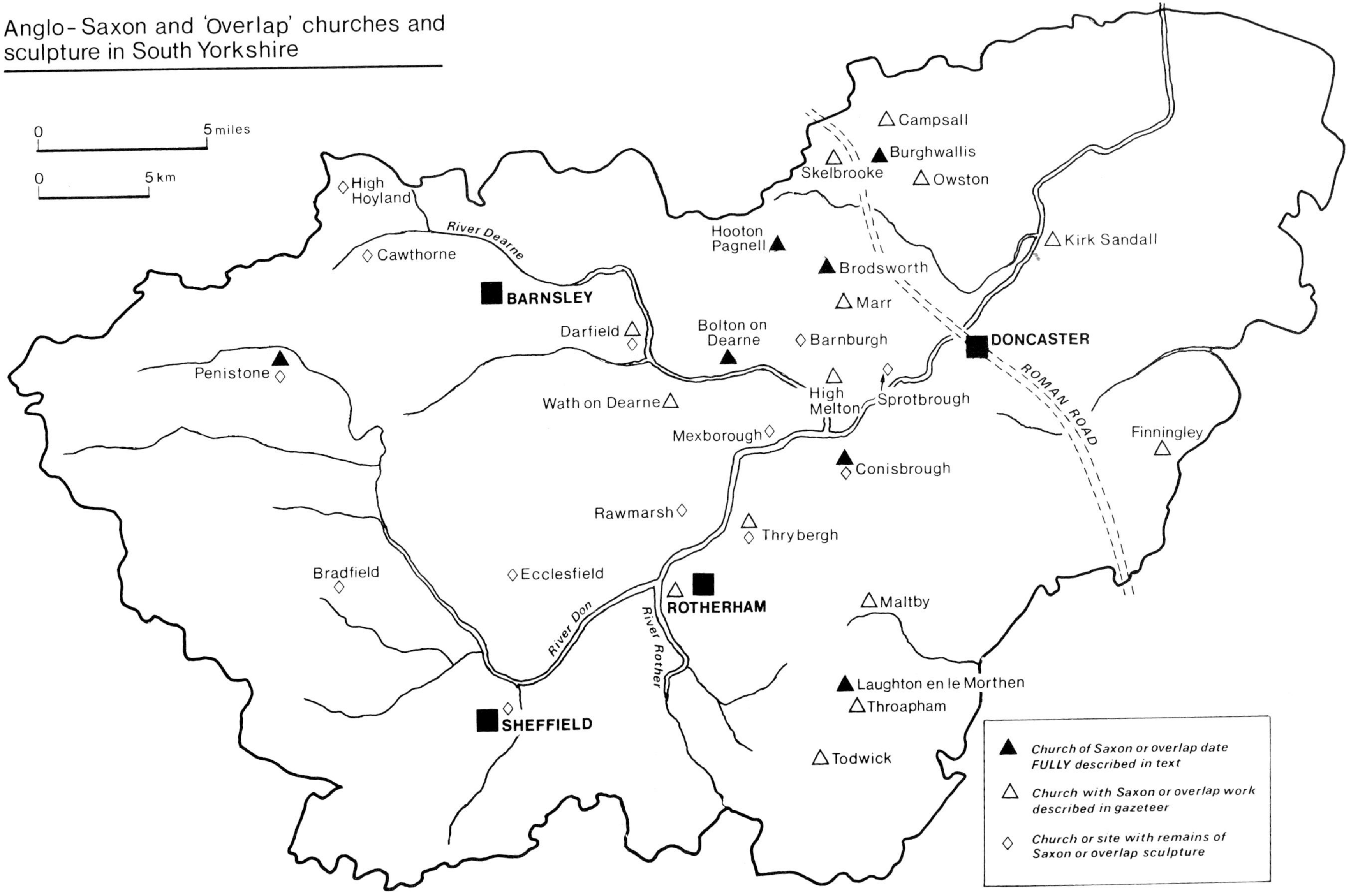

St. Andrew's Church, Bolton on Dearne

St. Andrew's church stands on the south side of the main street of Bolton-on-Dearne, an old village which has now virtually lost its identity amongst the 19th century industrial sprawl of the Dearne valley. Several writers have dismissed the church as of no real interest, "a poor unrestored little church"[1], and its importance as a pre-Conquest structure has only recently been recognised[2].

Only the nave survives of the pre-Conquest structure, the chancel, west tower and north aisle all being of later medieval date. The north chancel chapel in its present form was rebuilt in the 19th century and the vestry is an addition of the same date.

DESCRIPTION

THE SAXON NAVE

The nave is slightly trapezoidal in plan, c. 30 ft. 10 ins. (9.4 m.) long, the north wall 31 ft. 2 ins. (9.5 m.), the south wall 30 ft. 6 ins. (9.3 m.) and 19 ft. 9 ins. (6.02 m.) wide internally, with walls 2 ft. 9 ins. (0.85 m.) in thickness. The internal faces of the walls are plastered, and much of the north, east and west walls removed by the insertion of later arches. The exposed outer face of the south wall shows it to be of roughly-coursed sandstone, with massive long and short angle quoins. The south-east quoin, its upright long stones averaging 4 ft. (1.2 m.) in height and the intermediate short ones less than 1 ft. (0.3 m.) remains to a height of over 19 ft. 8 ins. (6.0 m.) (the pre-Conquest walls appear to have been at least 21ft. 4 ins. (6.5 m.) in overall height). The south-west quoin has been reconstructed above 9 ft. 10 ins. (3.0 m.) from ground level. A considerable section of the north-west quoin survives, to the north of the later tower. Here the upper parts of the quoining are intact but the base has been rebuilt.

The only early architectural features to survive are confined to the south wall. Near the centre of the wall is an original round-headed window. The outer opening of this, enriched by a shallow double rebate, is 2 ft. 8 ins. (0.82 m.) high and 1 ft. 1 in. (0.33 m.) wide, and cut in a single slab of sandstone 3 ft. 11 ins. (1.2 m.) by 3 ft. 3 ins. (1.0 m.). Internally the window splays to a width of just over 3 ft. 3 ins. (1.0 m.), all details of the rear-arch being obscured by plaster.

Externally, the remains of two early arches can be distinguished in the wall, although a combination of the decay of the stonework and later pointing and cement makes it somewhat difficult to perceive this. The head of each arch has been destroyed by a later window.

The western arch has been 6 ft. 11 ins. (2.1 m.) wide, its west jamb only 4 ft. 7 ins. (1.4 m.) from the end of the wall. Both jambs survive and appear to be built of stones laid alternately upright and flat (what has been termed 'Escomb fashion', from the well known Saxon church in County Durham where the north door is the type example of this technique). The impost blocks survive, and one voussoir of the arch on each side. The Saxon opening has been occupied by a

ST ANDREW'S CHURCH, BOLTON UPON DEARNE

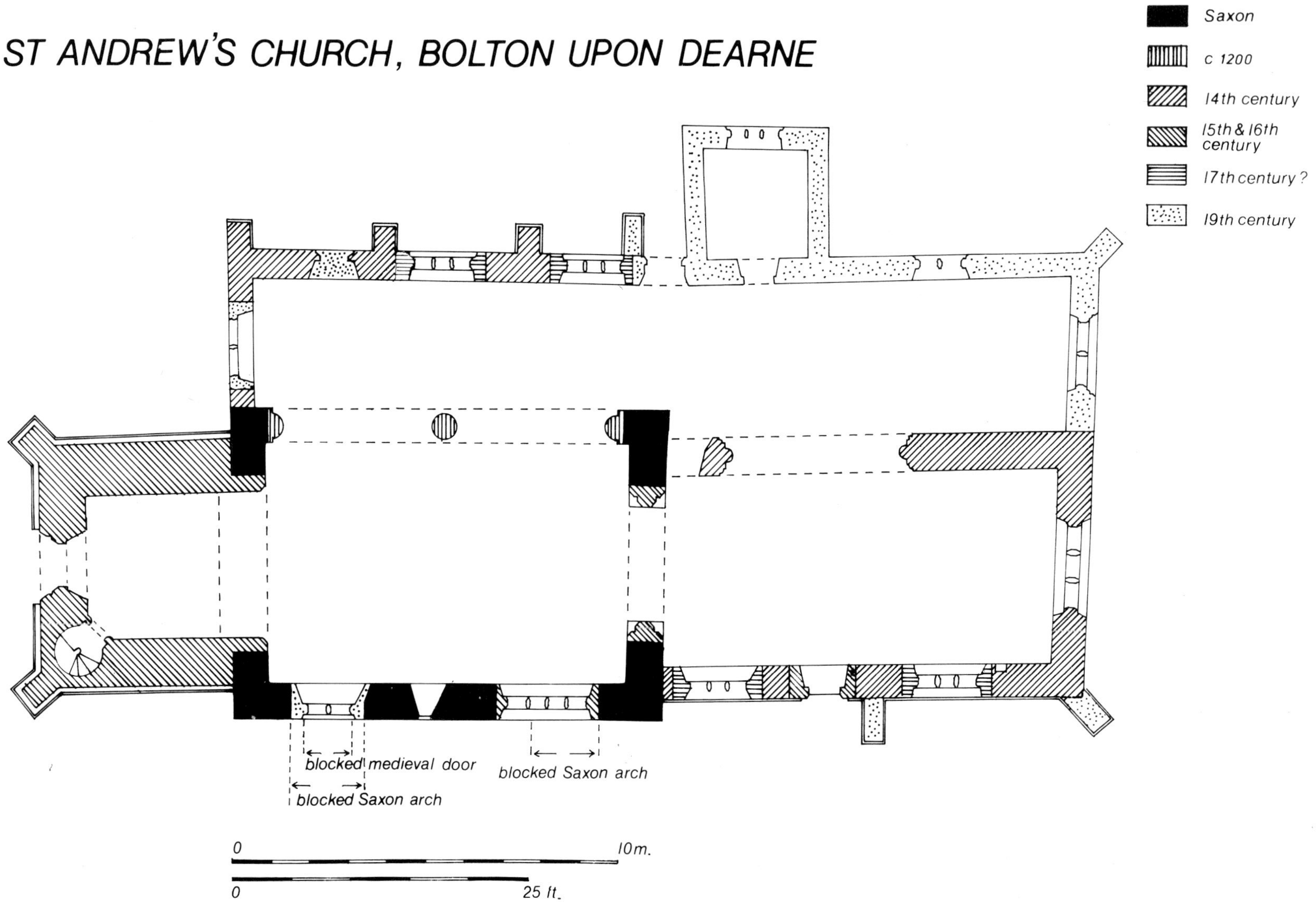

South Yorkshire County Archaeology Service 1981

narrower medieval door (as at Laughton-en-le-Morthen). Later on this too was blocked and the present two-light window was cut through the wall, destroying the heads of both earlier openings. Hunter, writing in 1831[3] states that "the circular arch over the principal entrance seems to belong to the original church", from this it appears that the south door remained intact and in use in his time.

ST ANDREW'S CHURCH, BOLTON UPON DEARNE

Anglo Saxon features in south wall of nave

The second early arch has its east jamb 5 ft. 6 ins. (1.67 m.) from the east end of the wall, and is 5 ft. 8 ins. (1.73 m.) wide. Less survives of the jambs here, but like those of the western arch they appear to have been built Escomb fashion (Taylor[4] notes the traces of this opening but not the rather more apparent remains of the western arch). The eastern jamb in addition bears a hint of what appears to be cut-back stripwork.

The eastern arch probably gave access to a porticus or side-chapel. From its position the western arch would most likely have served as the main south door of the church. A similar arrangement of south door and (presumed) porticus arch can be seen at Kirk Hammerton church between Harrogate and York.

Pre-Conquest masonry is also exposed on the external face of the east wall of the nave above the low-pitched roof of the later chancel. The partial rendering of this wall makes the interpretation of any features difficult, but indications survive of the steeply pitched roof of an earlier chancel, apparently somewhat narrower than its successor.

THE RE-USED FRIEZE

Although no other pre-Conquest masonry seems to survive *in situ* in any part of the church other than the nave, re-used in the late medieval tower are a series of blocks from what appears to have been a decorative frieze. This may conceivably be pre-Conquest work, although parallels of any date, Saxon or medieval, are not easy to find. Fourteen blocks survive, re-set into the internal faces of all four walls of the second stage of the tower (the ringing chamber). The frieze bears a simple pattern of raised lozenges, their vertical axes greater than their horizontal, each lozenge extending the full height 1 ft. 3 ins. (0.38 m.) of the block. The blocks have been re-set in a frieze form but not in their original order; one may terminate in a half-lozenge, whilst that adjacent commences the pattern with a complete motif.

THE DATE OF THE PRE-CONQUEST FABRIC

The nave at Bolton-on-Dearne differs from that at Conisbrough, the only other surviving nave definitely of Saxon date in the area, in two important particulars, its dimensions and its angle quoining.

The Bolton nave measures internally 30 ft. 1 in. (9.4 m.) by 19 ft. 8 ins. (6.02 m.), a length to breadth ratio of roughly 1:5, whereas Conisbrough is 44 ft. (13.4 m.) by 17 ft. 1 in. (5.2 m.), a ratio of 2:5. The angle quoins at Bolton are of classic long-and-short type, whilst those at Conisbrough are of the side-alternate variety.

A distinct group of Northumbrian Saxon churches has been recognised by several workers, characterised by naves of relatively long and narrow proportions[5] and the almost invariable use of side-alternate quoins[6]. Conisbrough appears to belong to this group, but Bolton on the other hand has a nave whose length to breadth ratio is much nearer the norm for English Anglo-Saxon naves[7] and one of the most northerly examples of long-and-short quoins.

Whilst comparison with other churches of the Northumbrian group suggests that Conisbrough is relatively early Saxon work (8th century), Bolton is more difficult to date. It is quite obviously the product of a different building tradition, and almost certainly later in date. Taylor[8] cites long-and-short quoining as being in use from the 9th century right up to the Norman Conquest.

The re-used frieze is a most unusual feature, with no real parallel in any English pre-Conquest church[9]. The lozenge pattern is reminiscent of some Norman sculpture (which often uses simple geometrical motifs) but again, close parallels are hard to find. Somewhat similar patterns on a smaller scale do occur in the South Yorkshire Overlap churches of Hooton Pagnell (incised decoration on impost of chancel arch) and Brodsworth (relief decoration on string course re-used as a set-back around the 13th century west tower). On the basis of these one might date the Bolton frieze, very tentatively, to the 11th century.

MEDIEVAL ALTERATIONS AND ENLARGEMENT

At present there are no architectural features visible in the church which fall in date between the Saxon nave and the north arcade of c. 1200. The writer of a Victorian pamphlet decrying local church restorations, 'Gaudens in Proelio', speaks of "some old Norman work ... which has been covered over with plaster"[10], but does not enlarge upon this statement.

The two-bay north arcade is an insertion dated by Pevsner[11] to c. 1200. The arches are pointed and of two orders, the inner chamfered and the outer square, carried on semicircular responds and a circular pier. The pier and responds have octagonal and semi-octagonal abaci, that of the pier having a crude attempt at a crocket at each angle.

The church was further enlarged in the 14th century, the chancel being rebuilt and the north aisle extended eastwards as a chapel. It seems likely that the walls of the aisle were rebuilt at this time as well.

The east window of the chancel, of three trefoil-headed lights with three large quatrefoils over beneath a pointed arch, although somewhat restored appears to be genuine early 14th century work. The simple trefoil-headed piscina recess at the east end of the south wall is also probably an original feature, although its arch is partly masked by modern panelling. The projecting bowl, much plastered over, appears to have been of semi-octagonal form.

The broad four-centred arch on the north side of the chancel also appears to be 14th century work, and may be dated by the record[12] of the founding of a chantry "on the north side of the church" in 1328. The arch is of two quadrant-moulded orders, the outer continued to the ground and the inner carried on semicircular responds with moulded capitals. The base of the eastern one has been cut away and that of the western is hidden by the present floor. To the west of the arch is a pointed doorway with a broad continuous chamfer towards the chapel.

The north and west walls of the north aisle also appear to be 14th century work, although much altered. The only dateable feature is the quadrant moulding of the blocked north door, only visible externally and heavily rendered over. Of the four stepped buttresses on the north of the aisle, the three western look to be medieval work, probably coeval with the wall.

The chancel arch in its simplicity is difficult to date, a rather tall and narrow pointed opening of two continuous chamfered orders stopped c. 3 ft. 3 ins. (1.0 m.) above the floor. The lack of imposts might suggest a 15th rather than a 14th century date.

The western tower built of gritstone ashlar appears to be a late medieval addition to the church, of 15th or even early 16th century date. Externally, string courses hollow-chamfered beneath divide the tower into three stages. These do not correspond to the internal floors the lower string being set considerably below the level of the ringing chamber floor. There is a tall plinth with typical Perpendicular convex mouldings. At each angle of the tower is a stepped diagonal buttress extending to just above the second string. The western buttresses rise from ground level, the eastern from the nave parapets.

The base of the tower opens to the nave by a tall pointed arch of two chamfered orders, the outer continued down the jambs to ground level towards the nave, the others simply dying into the wall. The west door has a round-headed arch of two continuous chamfered orders, and a hollow-chamfered hoodmould. Above is a window of three trefoil-headed lights with simple panel tracery over, under a pointed arch with a broad hollow chamfer of jambs and head. The lower of the string courses is carried up and over the head of the window as a hoodmould. In the south-west angle of the tower is a newel stair, entered by a small door with a flat-pointed Tudor arch with a simple chamfer of head and jambs, and lit by small rectangular loops.

The ringing chamber now has no windows, but the clock faces on north and south appear to occupy older openings with plain square-headed rear arches.

The belfry has a two-light opening in each wall. These have transoms at mid-height, uncusped arched heads to the main lights and the most basic of panel tracery beneath a pointed head, with a hollow chamfered hood. The lack of cusping suggests a late date, and the openings may be post-medieval reconstruction. There are some similarities to the belfry openings at All Hallows' Church, High Hoyland, where the tower is known to have been erected in 1679. Above the belfry openings is a third string course, and the tower is finished with an embattled parapet and crocketted angle pinnacles.

The large four-light window at the east end of the south wall of the nave bears some similarities to the belfry openings in that its main lights are uncusped and divided by a transom. The panel tracery beneath the four-centred arch of the window head here, however, has small trefoil-headed and cinquefoil-headed lights, and suggests that the window is genuine medieval work (probably a 15th century insertion) which has had the cusping of its main lights cut away at some stage.

The embattled nave parapet may also be 15th century in date. On the south side of the chancel is a priest's door with a four-centred arched head and a hollow-chamfered hoodmould, which again looks like 15th or early 16th century work.

POST MEDIEVAL ALTERATIONS

The church retains four windows of what Sir Stephen Glynne[13] termed "debased" style, simple square-headed openings divided by mullions into three lights. Two of these are on the south side of the chancel (the eastern of these differs from the others in having a shouldered rear arch) and two in the north wall of the north aisle. Windows of this type, which in most other local churches were removed by Victorian restorers, are difficult to date closely, but may perhaps be ascribed to the 17th or early 18th century.

The external walls of the church have seen a great deal of patching and repair. Blocks of stone showing horizontal tooling characteristic of early 19th century work are everywhere apparent, especially on the south side of the chancel where the upper half of the wall seems to have been completely refaced.

The walls of the north chapel appear to have been completely rebuilt in the first half of the 19th century, and the small vestry on the north is of the same date. The west window of the north aisle and the window at the west end of the south wall of the nave also appear to be early Victorian work.

NON-STRUCTURAL FEATURES OF INTEREST

'Gaudens in Proelio'[14] notes that when Bolton church was restored the old chancel screen was "demolished" and that the then rector "turned the old font into a fern pot, and also broke up what carved work remained in his church". The vicarage, in the garden of which one presumes the fern pot resided, has been moved at least twice since the 19th century and the font lost.

MEDIEVAL SEPULCHRAL MONUMENTS

Several medieval cross slab grave covers have been re-used in the church fabric. These are:-

(i) This is a fragmentary slab built into the internal wall of the newel staircase in the tower, just below the door into the ringing chamber. Part of a 'bracelet' cross head, probably early 13th century in date.

(ii) This is a slab built into the internal face of the east wall of the ringing chamber, just below the frieze and near the north-east corner. The stone shows an incised cross shaft and an emblem difficult to interpret.

(iii) This is a slab to the south of (ii) and shows a cross shaft with stepped calvary base. To the right of the shaft faint traces of an emblem, probably a chalice, suggesting that this stone formerly covered the grave of a priest.

(iv) A slab in the same wall, but low down at the north end. Plain Greek cross.

(v) A slab in the same wall at its south end, 4 ft. 11 ins. (1.5 m.) above the floor, showing cross shaft with stepped calvary base, sword on the right.

(vi) A cross slab built into the south wall of the ringing chamber, just above floor level and adjacent to the stair turret. Plain Greek cross with stepped calvary base and sword as on (v).

(vii) A stone in the north wall of the ringing chamber above the eastern section of the re-set frieze, showing a Greek cross with sword on right.

The plain Greek cross as seen on several of these stones is paralleled by slabs at Wath on Dearne, and is difficult to date specifically, occurring throughout the medieval period.

(viii) A slab built into the external north gable of the 19th century vestry, above the window. This is a sandstone block c. 2 ft. 0 ins. (0.6 m.) square bearing a simple cross paté within a circle. This stone may be a head-stone, of 12th century date.

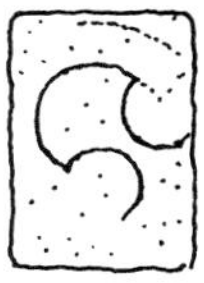

(i)

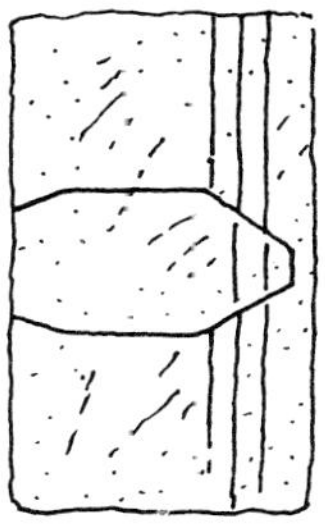

(ii)

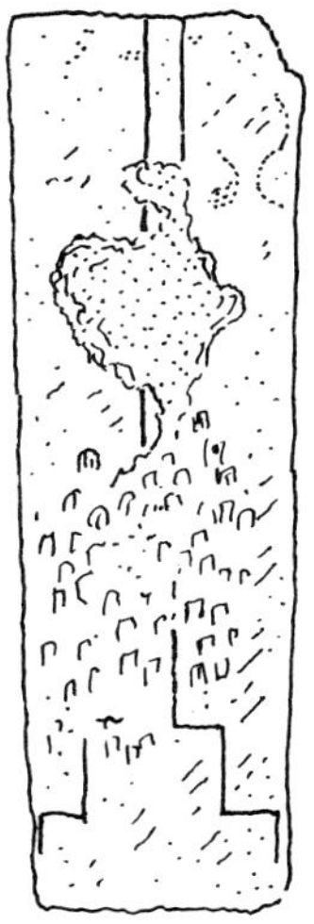

(iii)

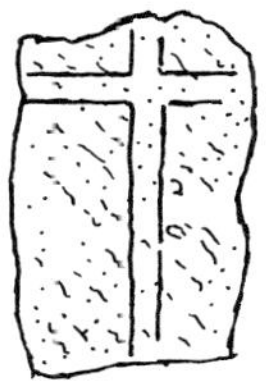

(iv)

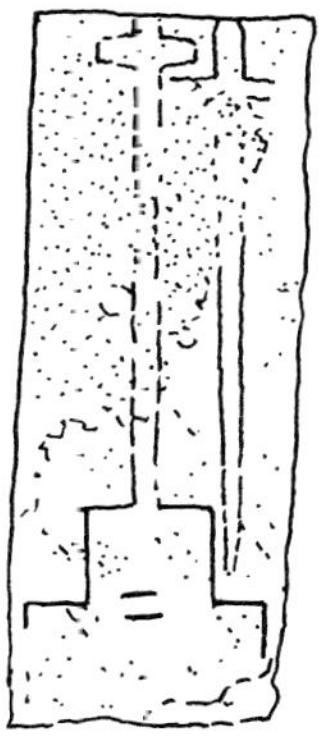

(v)

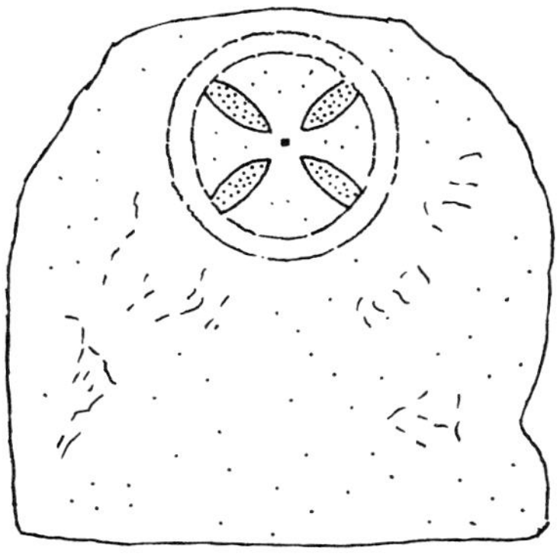

(viii)

0 50 cm.

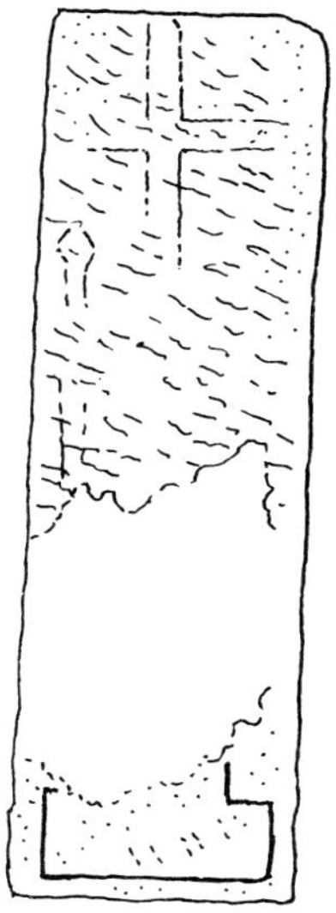

(vi)

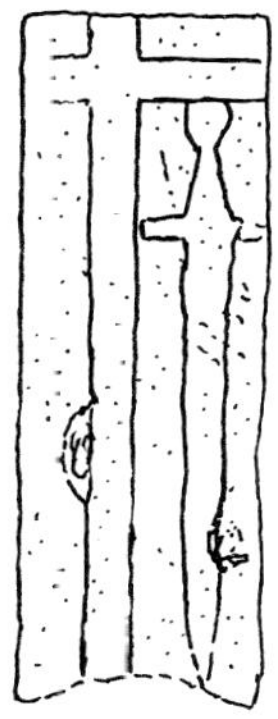

(vii)

REFERENCES

1	Morris, J. E.	*The West Riding of Yorkshire* (Little Guide Series) 115, 2nd edn. London: Methuen & Co. 1923
2	Pevsner, N.	*The Buildings of England: Yorkshire, the West Riding,* 619, 2nd edn. Harmondsworth: Penguin 1967
3	Hunter, J.	*South Yorkshire,* 1. 386. Nicholls & Son, 1831
4	Pevsner, N.	Op. cit, 119
5	Clapham, A. W.	*English Romanesque Architecture before the Conquest* 41, Oxford, 1930
6	Taylor, H. M.	*Anglo-Saxon Architecture,* III, 947, Cambridge: University Press, 1978
7	Taylor, H. M.	Ibid., 1032
8	Taylor, H. M.	Ibid., 1069
9	Taylor, H. M.	Private communication 26 Feb. 1981
10	'Gaudens in Proelio'	*Church Restoration,* 4. Sheffield: Pawson & Brailsford, 1867
11	Pevsner, N.	Op. cit, 117
12	Armitage, E. S.	*A Key to English Antiquities,* 224, Sheffield: William Townsend, 1897
13	Glynne, S.	Sir Stephen Glynne's Church Notes, *Yorkshire Archaeological Journal* XXIV, 210-211, 1917
14	'Gaudens in Proelio'	Op. cit., 4 - 5

St. Michael's Church, Brodsworth

St. Michael's church now stands on its own surrounded by the woodland to the east of Brodsworth Hall, a 19th century house whose predecessor lay alongside the churchyard. To the north of the church the ground falls steeply towards the narrow dry valley containing the scatter of houses which comprise the present village.

The church appears to have originally consisted of an aisleless nave, chancel and west tower of Overlap date, very similar in design to nearby Hooton Pagnell. In the later 12th century this small building was remodelled and enlarged, the area of the original tower being thrown into the nave to which a north aisle and a new western tower were added, and the chancel extended eastward. Later medieval additions included a chapel and vestry north of the chancel. In 1874 the church was restored and enlarged further, a south aisle and south chancel chapel being added.

THE EARLY CHURCH

This consisted of a nave 25 ft. 7 ins. (7.8 m.) by 18 ft. 6 ins. (5.65 m.) internally, with a west tower 14 ft. 1 in. (4.3 m.) by 16 ft. 5 ins. (5.0 m.). The nave north wall is 2 ft. 9 ins. (0.84 m.) thick and the north and west tower walls 3 ft. 6 ins. (1.06 m.), the outer face of nave and tower north walls being continuous without any structural division. Nothing survives of the original chancel but by analogy with Hooton Pagnell it might be expected to have been 9 ft. 10 ins. (3.0 m.) long and 13 ft. 9 ins. (4.2 m.) wide.

The fabric of the walls is of coursed rubble with the occasional course laid obliquely or in herringbone fashion. The western angle quoins of the original tower survive and are of side-alternate type, averaging 1 ft. 3 ins. (0.37 m.) in height.

The only original features to survive *in situ* are in the west wall of the former tower, now the west gable of the nave. Externally this shows a plain string course of square section c. 19 ft. 8 ins. (6.0 m.) above the present floor level, now only seen from the first floor chamber in the tower. The string in effect forms a set-back, projecting 1½ ins. (0.04 m.) from the wall face below and 6 ins. (0.16 m.) from that above. The string itself is 4½ ins. (0.12 m.) deep. Below the string and above the inserted late 12th century tower arch is a shallow recess in the external face of the wall which appears at first sight to be a blocked door or window. This is c. 4 ft. 5 ins. (1.35 m.) high and 1 ft. 6 ins. (0.47 m.) wide, with an irregular roughly pointed head. The sill of the recess appears to have been cut into by the top of the tower arch beneath.

On the east (internal) face of the wall is a confusion of joints, different masonry types and repairs due to recent subsidence damage, creating a picture almost impossible to interpret. The only architectural feature is four stones of the south jamb of an opening. If these do indicate the rear arch of the door or window seen on the other side of the wall a deep internal splay to a width of c. 7 ft. 5 ins. (2.25 m.) would be indicated. A quite distinct vertical break in the masonry does occur on the theoretical line of the north jamb of such an opening. Straight joints may indicate a narrower blocked opening lower down the wall, just above and to

ST. MICHAEL'S CHURCH, BRODSWORTH

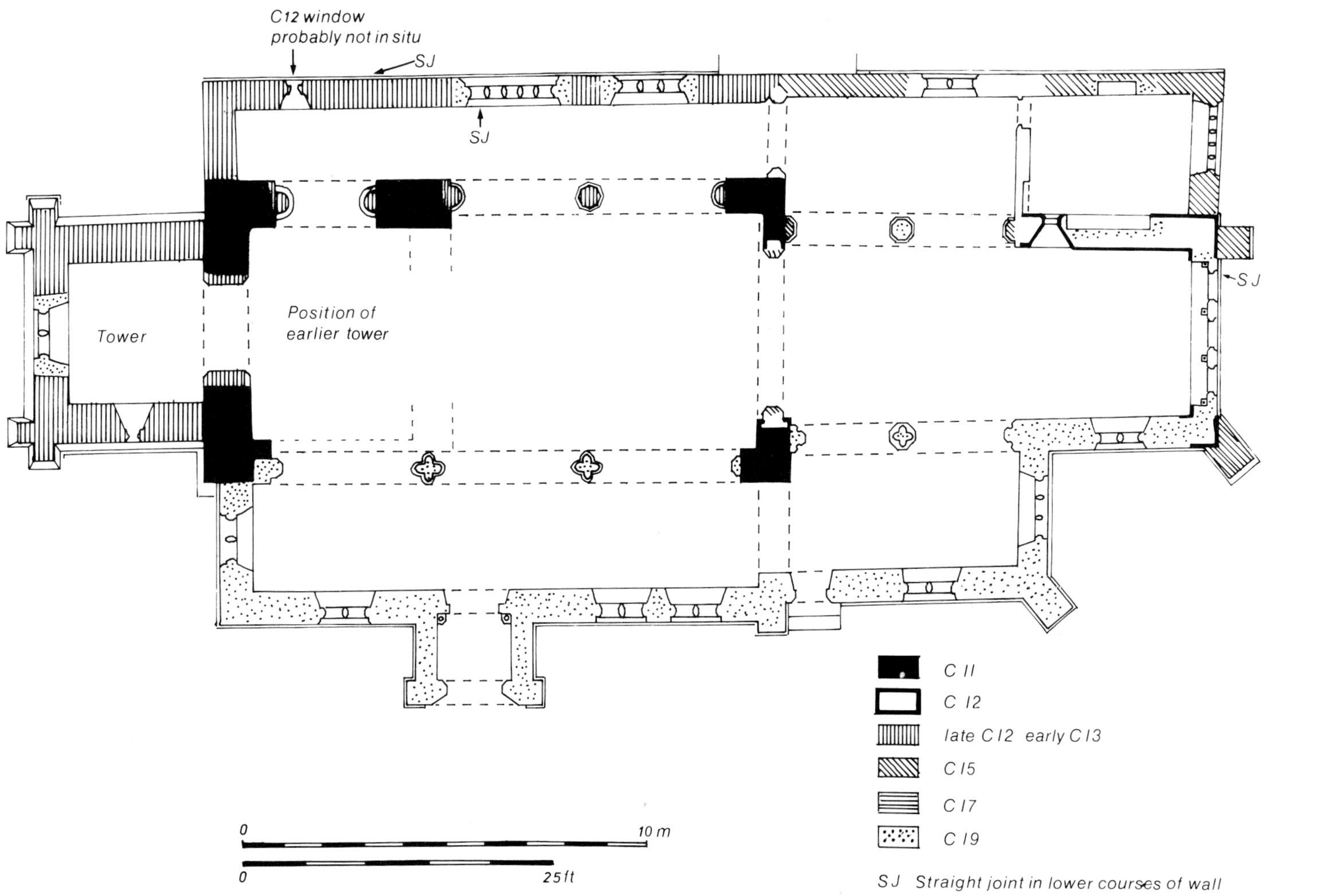

South Yorkshire County Archaeology Service 1981

the south of the south jamb of the tower arch.

It is by no means certain that either of these openings is an early feature. The external face of the wall is plastered, and thus cannot be examined in detail. The irregular form of the opening seen on that side of the wall might hint at it being a late insertion, perhaps connected with the gallery removed from the west end of the nave in 1874. A piece of brick built into its sill does not augur for an early date. However a plan of the gallery in its 19th century form[1] does not show any opening through the west wall of the nave above the tower arch.

The north wall of the former tower, now pierced by a late 12th century arch to the aisle, does not show any original features. The toothing of the removed east wall of the tower is quite apparent, as is the step back in thickness from tower to nave wall. The corresponding step back on the south is evident on the 1874 plan[2], but on this side the wall was completely removed to make way for the 19th century arcade. Built into the toothing for the north end of the removed east wall of the tower, 10 ft. 8 ins. (3.26 m.) above floor level, is a stone 3 ft. 5 ins. (1.05 m.) long and 5 ins. (0.12 m.) high, chamfered beneath, which might conceivably have been an impost block from the removed tower arch.

Internal Elevation of the West Wall of the Nave (drawn from photographs)

LATE 12th TO EARLY 13th CENTURY REMODELLING

Towards the end of the 12th century the church was extended considerably, its floor area being virtually doubled.

The added north aisle opens to the nave by an arcade of three arches, the western arch, cut through the thicker wall of the former tower, being separated from the eastern pair by 6 ft. 0 in. (1.8 m.) of solid walling. The western arch has responds consisting of heavy half-cylinders with overhanging square abaci, carrying a pointed arch which is entirely of 19th century date, the original having been destroyed by the stair to the western gallery, removed in 1874. The capitals of the responds of the eastern arches are of similar form but rather taller, the change

Reconstructed perspective impressions

The 11th century church with timber belfry

The church c. 1200, after addition of the present tower and the north aisle

The church today, showing the tower heightened later in the medieval period and the north aisle extended alongside the chancel

in section from half-cylinder to square abacus being accomplished less abruptly. The bases of all four responds and of the pillar carrying the eastern arches are all of moulded hold-water form.

The pillar is octagonal and carries an octagonal capital, enriched with decoration of a hybrid form related to both scallop and waterleaf designs. The two western faces have trefoiled leaves, less fully developed on the south and barely suggested to north and east. The eastern arches themselves are pointed and of two orders, the inner chamfered and the outer square.

The walls of the north aisle appear to have suffered much rebuilding. One small round-headed window, deeply splayed internally, survives near the west end of the north wall. Its outer opening, heavily rendered over, appears to have a rebate on its external face. This rather suggests that the window has been removed at some stage and re-set into the wall the wrong way round. The square-headed rear arch also suggests that this is not an *in situ* Norman piece.

A 12th century chevron-moulded voussoir built into the external face of the wall beneath the window also suggests that there has been some disturbance. It may be derived from a former north door, whose position may be indicated by one or other of two straight joints seen in the lower courses of the wall, one on the external face 15 ft. 3 ins. (4.65 m.) from the north-west corner and one internally 19 ft. 0 ins. (5.8 m.) from the corner.

The chancel was probably extended eastwards in the 12th century. The Norman chancel arch of which some remains survive probably dates from this remodelling. It has been considerably wider, c. 13 ft. 2 ins. (4.0 m.) as opposed to 10 ft. 10 ins. (3.3 m.), than that at Hooton Pagnell which can be assumed to date from the first phase of work there, roughly contemporary with the first phase at Brodsworth. At Brodsworth the south jamb of the 12th century arch survives, visible from the west only, a plain square-section jamb with a rather mutilated square impost. Four voussoirs of what was apparently a semicircular arch remain *in situ* above. The later (15th century?) chancel arch has its inner order set within the old jambs, and its outer order resting on the surviving voussoirs of the older arch. A similar fragment of the 12th century arch survives on the north but here the west face of the wall has been cut back later, destroying the impost. However the cut-back blocks survive, indicating that the impost block was carried back as a string across the west face of the wall.

Other late 12th century remains survive in the east half of the north wall, and possibly the lower part of the east gable. The former contains a round-headed Norman or Transitional window, now opening into the vestry, and has original string courses on both faces. The window is quite tall and wide and deeply splayed internally. The string courses, at window sill level, are chamfered above and below. That on the internal face of the wall has been heavily retooled.

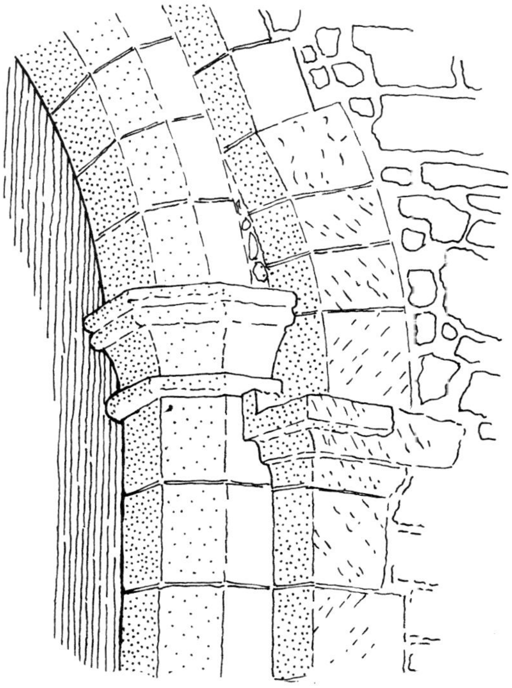

South Jamb of Chancel Arch

Externally, the 12th century string can be seen to turn to continue across the east gable, but does not re-emerge from behind the added buttress just short of the north end of the wall. Internally, a string of similar section runs just below the sills of the present windows which are 19th century in date. This may be 12th century work re-set; the windows break the projected line of the external string. In the external face of the wall, below the north jamb of the northernmost window is a distinct straight joint, a feature hard to explain.

The present western tower, 10 ft. 10 ins. (3.3 m.) square internally, has walls 3 ft. 2 ins. (0.95 m.) in thickness and is divided externally into three stages by chamfered set backs. Pairs of stepped buttresses at the western angles rise to just below the upper set back. On the south the chamfered face of this upper set back bears a relief diaper pattern of lozenges, a motif continued down the vertical western faces of the coping stones of the west gable of the nave on both sides of the tower. The set back on the west side of the tower is plain. That on the north bears some remains of a zigzag pattern in lower relief, this time on the vertical rather than on the chamfered face. These pieces of ornament, and the kneeler stone at the south-west angle of the nave which bears a line of raised balls, appear to be re-used work.

The ground floor of the tower opens onto the nave by a pointed arch, 6 ft. 11 ins. (2.11 m.) wide and 9 ft. 9 ins. (2.98 m.) high, with a simple narrow chamfer of jambs and head, and square impost blocks chamfered beneath. On the south is a small lancet window, deeply splayed internally, and on the west a two-light window of 19th century date.

The second stage of the tower, reached by a modern ladder, is lit by a single square-headed loop on the south.

The third (belfry) stage of the tower was raised later in the medieval period. The original belfry was barely half the present height, with a single rather narrow opening in each wall directly above the set back. Only the jambs and sills of these survive, beneath the sills of their later replacements.

It is possible that the various enlargements and alterations detailed above are the work of two or more separate phases. Pevsner[3] dates the western arch of the north arcade to the late 12th century and the eastern arches to the early 13th. However he failed to unravel the evidence for the early tower and dates the chancel east lancets and nave south door to the 13th century when they are quite plainly Victorian work. The remains of the chancel arch and surviving chancel window are distinctly Norman work of the later 12th century. The west tower looks as if it may be a little later, Transitional in style, and may be ascribable to the first years of the 13th century.

LATER MEDIEVAL ALTERATIONS

The heightening of the west tower is difficult to date. The belfry openings, ascribed by Pevsner[4] to the 13th century, are of unusual form and could well be 14th or 15th century work. Each consists of two lights beneath an enclosing arch with a single broad chamfer. To north, south and west the enclosing arch is of four-centred form, and the individual lights have semi-circular, almost elliptical, heads. On the south some weathered carving in the spandrel above the two lights is difficult to interpret; some form of flower or rosette on the right is fairly clear. On the west the spandrel is partly hidden by rendering, through which traces of what may be a quatrefoil piercing can be seen. On the north any design is hidden by rendering. The eastern opening is the most peculiar. The enclosing arch is semicircular and the two lights have angular pointed heads. The carving in the spandrel shows a six-pointed Star of David on the left and a multi-petalled flower on the right. This can be more easily seen through binoculars.

The tower parapet, with the base of a removed pinnacle at each angle, and hollow-chamfered string just below look as if they may be late medieval work, but are not shown on a painting of the church made prior to 1860[5] which depicts the tower with a squat pyramidal roof and a crocketted pinnacle at each corner.

In the 15th century the chancel arch was remodelled and a chapel and vestry added on the north side of the chancel. The chancel arch, as recast, is pointed and of two orders, the inner chamfered and the outer square. The inner order rests on semi-octagonal responds with moulded capitals, the mouldings being continued on the east around the outer order. On the west the outer order rests on the jambs and some voussoirs of the 12th century arch, as has already been described.

The north chapel before 1874 opened to the chancel by "a very wide pointed arch upon octagonal shafts"[6], replaced by a two bay arcade. The old responds appear to have been re-used, and are semi-octagonal with moulded capitals and bases rather similar to those of the chancel arch.

The chapel opens to the north aisle of the nave by a peculiar stilted arch which appears 19th century in its present form.

The vestry, to the east of the chapel, prior to 1874 was entered from the chancel by a "flattened trefoil-headed door"[7] beneath the Norman window. No evidence of this is now visible (the wall is plastered on both sides) and the present vestry door, from the chapel, is modern. The vestry has a square-headed window of five narrow lights on the east which at first sight looks like 16th or 17th century work, but could possibly be coeval with the vestry and chapel.

The stepped buttress near the north end of the east wall of the chancel and the diagonal buttress at its south-east corner may also be 15th century work.

POST-MEDIEVAL ALTERATIONS

The majority of the windows of the church existing prior to the 1874 restoration appear to have been work of the preceeding two centuries.

A painting of the church from the south-east made prior to 1860[8] shows in the south wall of the nave, from west to east, a broad lancet, a segmental-headed door with a raised keystone (18th century?) and a three-light window with intersecting tracery beneath a four-centred head (perhaps an 18th or 19th century adaptation of a 15th century feature). The wall has a crenellated parapet which appears to have been replaced on the present wall and which may have been of 15th century date. The chancel shows round-headed Georgian windows to south and east, the former with a square-headed door beneath it. Sir Stephen Glynne, writing in 1860[9] states "the windows north and south of the nave are of three lights without foliation, and doubtful period, except one late square-headed one".

By 1874 some Gothic features had been re-introduced. The Georgian east window had been replaced by the present three lancets and the single light window near the west end of the south wall of the nave by one of three lights. A south porch had been added. The 1874 plan[10] shows the three windows on the north side of the aisle and that on the north of the chancel chapel as all of the same dimensions as at present. The westernmost is the small 12th century loop. The next two windows now look totally 19th century work, both square-headed, the first of five cinquefoil-headed lights, the second of three trefoil-headed lights. The chapel window, a plain square-headed opening divided into two lights by a central mullion, may be a surviving 17th century feature.

A gallery or loft, probably that at the west end of the nave, is known to have been erected in 1695[11]. In 1874 this western gallery was approached by a stair at the west end of the north

aisle and a door cut through the head of the westernmost arch of the arcade. A second gallery, the children's gallery, was set over the north chapel. It is quite possible that the abnormally wide arch here was a post-medieval reconstruction to make room for this.
In 1874 the church suffered a fairly comprehensive restoration. The south walls of nave and chancel were completely destroyed, a south aisle being added to the nave and a two-bay chapel to the chancel. More recently mining subsidence has occasioned extensive damage to the church, and the building is now heavily propped both inside and out.

NON-STRUCTURAL FEATURES OF INTEREST

THE FONT

The Font, beneath the tower, has a plain and heavy octagonal bowl set upon a shaft of the same section which rises from a square plinth. Lack of detail makes dating difficult. It is almost certainly a medieval piece, perhaps of the 14th or 15th century.

MEDIEVAL SEPULCHRAL MONUMENTS

Brodsworth church has one of the most extensive collections of medieval cross slab grave covers in South Yorkshire comprising:-

(i) A well preserved cross slab floor stone set in the floor of the nave, near the east end of the central aisle. Foliated cross with coats of arms. Rim inscription to Richard de Pickburn and Joanna his wife, who died on the 7th Ides of October (i.e. 9th October) 1421.

(ii) Part of a cross slab floor stone, very worn, to west of (i). Cross shaft with chalice on left and book on right, and remnants of rim inscription including the date 1438 (?).

(iii) In the floor of the north aisle, a very worn slab with traces of two cross shafts. Such double slabs are uncommon - the only other example so far recorded in the county is at Barnburgh.

(iv) A smaller slab standing beside (v), having a round-leaf bracelet cross with shears to left of the shaft, early 13th century.

(v) A slab standing beside (iv) and with a cross of very similar form. Sword wound with sword-belt on left of shaft.

(i) 0 50 cm

(vi) Standing upright at the west end of the north aisle is a slab showing an ornate cross head in relief with chalice on stem below. 14th century.

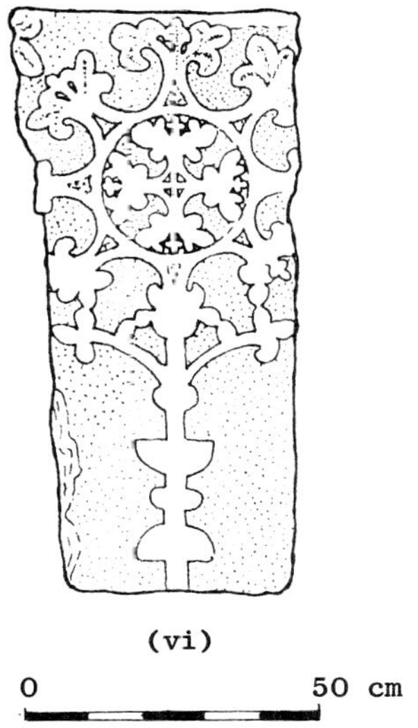

(vi)

(vii) Part of a slab forming the west half of the internal sill of the window of the north chancel chapel. Round-leaf bracelet head with open book to left of shaft. Early 13th century.

(viii) A fragment with pair of shears forms the east half of same window sill.

(ix) In floor of north chancel chapel, a slab showing a cross shaft with stepped Calvary base.

(x) A slab built into the internal face of the north wall of the chancel chapel, above the two-light window. Cross with 'ivy-leaf' head and sword on left of shaft. Early 14th century.

(xi) Part of a slab now forming part of the internal sill of the east window of the vestry. Round-leaf bracelet head with shears to left of shaft.

(xii) Part of a slab in the same window sill. 'Ivy-leaf' cross head, shears on left of shaft.

(xiii) Built into the interior of the south wall of the vestry, showing round-leaf bracelets set on a Greek cross, early 13th century.

(xiv) Beside (xiii) is a small slab showing a round-leaf bracelet head, and sword on the left of the shaft. Early 13th century.

(xv) Beside (xiv) head of a slab, with 'ivy-leaf' cross. Early 14th century.

(xvi) A fragment built into the interior of the west wall of the vestry. Small Maltese cross set inside a circle. Possibly a headstone, or even a consecration cross. 12th century (?).

(xvii) A fragment of a cross head built into the wall above the present south door. Greek cross with bracelets, early 13th century (?).

(xviii) Below and to the left of (xvii). Part of a small headstone with a much eroded cross paté. 12th century (?).

(xix) Below and to the right of (xvii). Similar to (xviii).

(xx) A fragment built into the external face of the north wall of the vestry, 3 ft. 3 ins. (1.0 m.) above ground level near the east end of the wall. Cross shaft with stepped Calvary base and sword on the left.

CARVED STONES

(a) A slab re-used as the base of the north jamb of the tower arch, on the west side of the wall. This is probably a coped grave slab, but only a small portion of one sloping face is exposed, showing a roll moulding on the edge and a scroll pattern with foliage. Perhaps 12th century work.

(b) What appears to have been a corbel to carry a roof truss, set in the internal face of the north wall of the north chancel chapel above and to the east of the two-light window. An angel, now headless, bearing a shield with three of the emblems of the Passion, the scourging-post, the spear, and a rod.

THE PULPIT

The pulpit is dated 1696, with carving of cherubs' heads, garlands etc. typical of that date.

REFERENCES

1.	1874 Plan	Plan with Faculty Ref. 1874/3, Borthwick Institute of Historical Research, York
2.	1874 Plan	Ibid.
3.	Pevsner, N.	*The Buildings of England: Yorkshire, the West Riding,* 148. 2nd edn. Harmondsworth: Penguin 1967
4.	Pevsner, N.	Ibid.
5.	Pre-1860 Painting	
6.	Glynne, S.	Sir Stephen Glynne's Church Notes, *Yorkshire Archaeological Journal* XV, 498-499, 189
7.	Glynne, S.	Ibid.
8.	Pre-1860 Painting	Op. cit.
9.	Glynne, S.	Op. cit.
10.	1874 Plan	Op. cit.
11.	1695 Loft	Faculty 1695/2, Borthwick Institute of Historical Research, York

St. Helen's Church, Burghwallis

St. Helen's church stands at the east end of the village of Burghwallis, 5 miles (8 km.) north-west of Doncaster, alongside Burghwallis Hall, a large house mostly Victorian in style but incorporating some 16th century work, the former seat of the Gascoigne and Anne families.
The church has a simple plan of nave, chancel and west tower, with a south porch and an organ chamber, now the vestry, north of the chancel. The nave and western section of the chancel are certainly of pre-Conquest or Overlap date. The tower is a later addition, still showing some Saxo-Norman characteristics. The date of the eastern extension of the chancel is problematic. Several windows and the south porch are later medieval work. The organ chamber and other windows are of the 19th century.

THE EARLY CHURCH

THE NAVE

The nave is a parallelogram in plan, measuring c. 33 ft. 10 ins. (10.3 m.) by 19 ft. 0 ins. (5.8 m.) internally, with walls 2 ft. 7 ins. (0.8 m.) in thickness. The angle quoins are of a megalithic side-alternate type, and the south wall is mostly of well-coursed herringbone work, incorporating a few larger blocks. The north wall has herringbone in the lower 5 ft. 0 ins. (1.5 m.) only, with semi-coursed rubble above suggesting that this part of the wall has been rebuilt. This is also borne out by the north-west quoin, which above four large blocks has been rebuilt in smaller stone. A little of the herringbone work on the south may be spurious, since an area of this type of masonry occupied the position of a possibly 18th century window above the porch, shown on an elevation of the wall made before the 1883 restoration[1]. The base of the south wall is formed by a course of large reddish blocks, set on a plain square plinth, now just below turf level, and exposed only in places. Both base course and plinth are continued along the south wall of the chancel.
In the nave walls the only opening which appears likely to be original work is the south door. This has plain square-section jambs cut straight through the wall, and rebated only on the inner face of the wall for a door hung in this rather unusual position. The head of the door has been altered towards the end of the medieval period. The plain square impost blocks which do not overhang the jambs now carry a flat four-centred head cut from a single stone much lighter in colour than the reddish imposts and voussoirs of the original arch which remain above. This is more segmental in shape than semicircular. The jamb stones look to be entirely 19th century restoration. The way in which this doorway is cut straight through the wall (assuming that the present form duplicates the original), and the way in which the door is hung on the inner face, are suggestive of an Anglo-Saxon date[2].
The blocked north doorway is visible only externally, the internal walls of the church being plastered , and its east jamb is obscured by a 19th century buttress. Both west jamb, composed of stones of no great size, and square head, cut in a comparatively light lintel, show a neat

ST. HELENS CHURCH, BURGHWALLIS

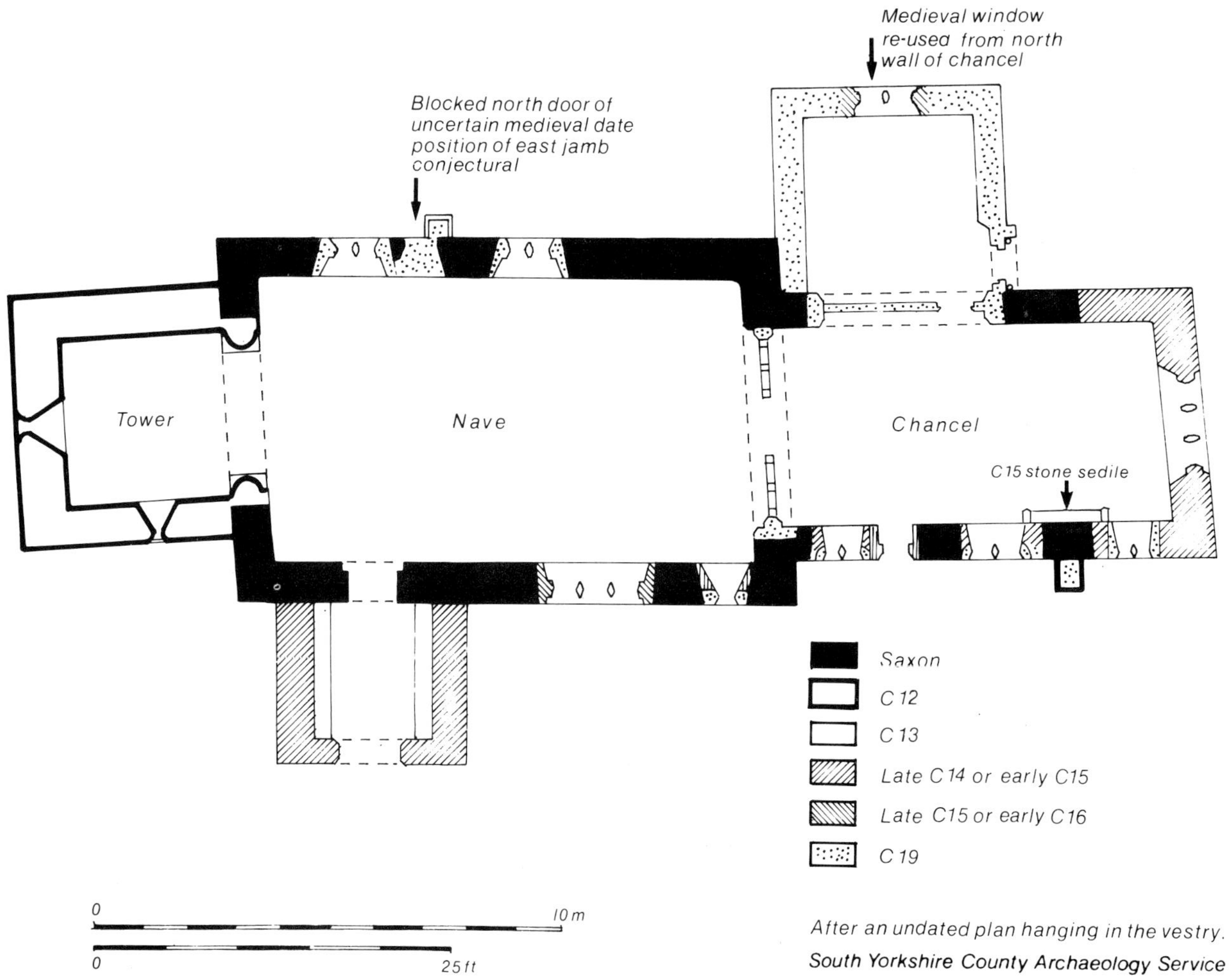

After an undated plan hanging in the vestry.
South Yorkshire County Archaeology Service 1981

chamfer. There is no feature to suggest that this very plain opening is early, and it may well be late medieval work.

On the external face of the west wall of the nave, just to the south of the south face of the tower, is a small stone set vertically, adjacent to a very large square block, its line continued downwards by a possible straight joint. At first sight this appears to be the south jamb of an opening blocked by the addition of the tower, but insufficient is exposed for a firm conclusion to be made.

THE CHANCEL

The present chancel measures internally 26 ft. 3 ins. (8.0 m.) by 13 ft. 5 ins. (4.1 m.). The exact line of the east end before extension is not quite clear but it would appear that the early chancel must have been c. 18 ft. 8 ins. (5.7 m.) in length. The south wall of the original chancel is of herringbone fabric, with an admixture of larger blocks of reddish stone, especially towards the west end of the wall. Three of these stones at the extreme west end of the wall are actually shaped to the re-entrant angle with the east wall of the nave. The herringbone masonry and base course of red stone both terminate roughly on the line of a 19th century buttress. No original angle quoins survive here, and it seems possible that they have been moved to the present east end. Taylor and Taylor[3] imply that they consider the present eastern quoins original, and also that the chancel has been extended, but do not indicate that the quoins have been moved.

The west part of the north wall of the chancel is now covered by the 19th century organ chamber. To the east of this, only slight indications of a break in masonry can be seen (the extension is probably marked by the use of large squared blocks at mid-wall height). The earlier wall west of this does not show any herringbone, but has been patched and perhaps partly refaced in the 19th century. The 1883 elevation [4] does show a break in the wall here, and labels the eastern section "an old addition".

No remains of early openings survive in the chancel. The priest's door on the south appears to be an insertion, and its head is cut from two stones rather than being "monolithic" as the Taylors record.

THE DATE OF THE NAVE AND CHANCEL

Herringbone work, so notable a feature of Burghwallis, has occasioned much academic controversy. Early workers thought it a sure indicator of pre-Conquest work, but Baldwin Brown in 1925[5] regarded it as a purely Norman innovation. More recently Taylor and Taylor[6] have demonstrated that herringbone or 'oblique coursing' is not characteristic of any one period, but was used by the Romans, Anglo-Saxons and Normans.

The megalithic side-alternate quoins at Burghwallis are a better indication of pre-Conquest work but do not allow a more specific dating. The combination here of this quoin form with herringbone fabric is apparently unique[7]. Although the church has previously been described as Norman[8] or even Transitional[9], the Taylors class it as of Saxon period 'C' (950 - 1100) on the evidence of its simple plan, plain square plinth, quoins and wall thickness. The form of the south door would seem to be additional evidence to their conclusion.

THE TOWER

The tower is 11 ft. 2 ins. (3.4 m.) square internally with walls 2 ft. 11 ins. (0.9 m.) thick. The manner in which its east wall is built over the west end of the nave, the fact that its side walls are not bonded into the nave wall, and the marked difference in masonry type between nave and tower all make it plain that the tower is a later addition.

The tower is in three stages, divided externally by string courses chamfered below forming slight set-backs. At the base of the walls is quite a tall chamfered plinth, and the walling is of coursed rubble with a scatter of larger blocks, often of reddish stone. The angle quoins are of side-alternate type, but much smaller than those of the nave. Unlike those of the nave, they do not utilise any of the red stone.

An area of large blocks on the west side of the lowest stage has been interpreted as "an indistinct vestige of a blocked west doorway",[10] but the coursing of the blocks across virtually the whole wall suggests otherwise. Just beneath the string course marking the base of the second stage are single-light windows to north and west. These have round-headed openings chamfered externally and deeply splayed internally. Their rear arches appear largely 19th century restoration.

The tower arch has apparently been reconstructed at some time. Its responds are broad half cylinders rising to heavy square abaci, the faces of which are simply decorated with a pair of incised lines. The arch itself does not fit the responds, being quite sharply pointed and of two orders, the inner chamfered and the outer square.

The second stage of the tower has on its east side a doorway, set considerably south of centre and now opening just under the roof of the nave. This has a plain round-headed arch 5 ft. 3 ins. (1.6 m.) high and 2 ft. 0 ins. (0.6 m.) wide, cut straight through the wall without any rebate. An internal set back on both north and south walls just above the level of the head of this door appears to indicate the position of a former floor. Set just above this, in the north wall, is an unusual window consisting of a circular oculus cut in a single square slab, splaying internally to a square-headed rear arch which appears totally 19th century work.

The belfry stage has two-light openings in each wall. Each light has a pointed lancet head, the outer jamb square and the division between the lights formed by twin cylindrical shafts, one behind the other, carrying a through-stone capital. On the east the inner shaft is replaced by a thin limestone slab.

THE DATE OF THE TOWER

Although obviously an addition, the tower retains some features indicative of pre-Conquest influence if not of actual pre-Conquest date. The high level doorway, both in its position and in the manner in which it is cut straight through the wall, is very suggestive of Saxon work. Its jambs do not have through-stones (a common pre-Conquest form) as such, but nowhere do more than two blocks suffice to line the opening. Many pre-Conquest towers in the North of England have such high level doorways which presumably gave access to chambers above the nave.

The monolithic circular window on the north side of the second stage of the tower is another feature of pre-Conquest form, but it appears highly unlikely that it is *in situ*. Elevations of the church made

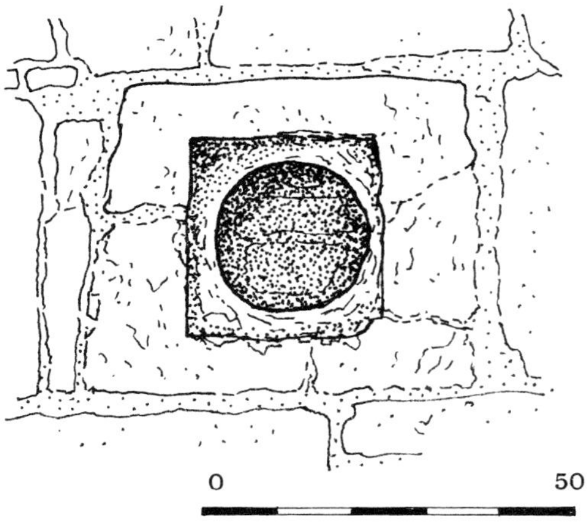

Oculus window re-used in the north wall of the chancel, former inner face.

in 1883[11] do not show any window here, or any proposal to insert such a window during the restoration. The position of the window, only a few inches above an old floor level, would be very unusual if it were ancient, and the present square-headed rear arch is certainly recent. It seems unlikely that this oculus window was discovered in 1883 in some other part of the church and moved to its present position. It may have come from the section of the north wall of the chancel removed when the organ chamber was added. There is in fact a second oculus window built into the remaining section of this wall east of the organ chamber.

Returning to the *in situ* features of the tower, the responds of the tower arch and the two windows of the lower stage are of conventional 12th century type. The tower arch itself must have been reconstructed in the 13th or 14th century. The belfry openings are a most puzzling feature, basically pre-Conquest in overall form but with twin shafts between the lights rather than single, and with pointed, that is 13th century style, heads. It almost looks as if we are dealing not with Saxo-Norman Overlap but with Saxo-Early English.

The Taylors regard the tower as "probably post-Conquest",[12] and on the balance of evidence this seems most likely. It is conceivable that the high level doorway may be a survival from an earlier tower or western annexe, although such features are not unknown in post-Conquest towers.

THE EXTENSION OF THE CHANCEL

At the end of the 14th or early in the 15th century the east end of the chancel was extended by a little over 6 ft. 7 ins. (2.0 m.). The new east gable was constructed of large ashlar blocks of white Magnesian Limestone, coursed in with the side-alternate angle quoining. These quoins are of comparable size with the early quoins of the nave, and it has been suggested [13] that they are in fact the original chancel quoins moved eastward. However, they differ from the nave quoins in being of much more regular size and in being all of white limestone, whereas the nave quoins are a mixture of white and red.

Disturbance of the outer face of the east wall beneath the east window, and the manner in which the jamb stones of the window are not coursed in with the adjacent walling, make it appear as if the window is an insertion in an earlier wall. However, on consulting the 1883 drawings[14] the situation is made clear; when the church was restored, the pitch of nave and chancel roofs were raised, thus necessitating a heightening of the east gable. So as to retain the proportions of the east end, the east window was removed and re-set higher in the wall.

The window itself is of three trefoil-headed lights with simple panel tracery over, under a four-centred arch with a hollow-chamfered hoodmould both inside and out, the internal hoodmould having been retooled in the 19th century. Both window and the ashlar masonry of the gable are paralleled in the east gable of the chapel of Campsall Old Rectory, 1¼ miles (2 km.) to the north-east, which may well have been a work of the same mason.

The side walls of the extension are not of the same ashlar as the east gable, but are constructed of a mixture of rubble and larger blocks, probably re-used material from the earlier east end. The north wall incorporates a group of very large squared blocks at c. 5 ft. 0 ins. (1.5 m.) above ground level. One of these is a reddish slab pierced by an oculus window of precisely similar form to that in the tower. This, and the example now in the tower, may have lit the original east end.

THE 13th AND 14th CENTURIES

The reconstruction of the tower arch to a pointed form may be 13th century work. The lancet window at the east end of the south wall of the nave also appears to be work of this period, although in its present form the outer opening is entirely 19th century restoration. Prior to 1883[15] there was a narrow square-headed light here. Parts of the shouldered rear arch appear ancient.

The chancel arch, although entirely Victorian in its present form, may also have been reconstructed in the 13th or 14th century. The pointed arch of two orders, the inner chamfered, the outer chamfered to the nave but square to the chancel, set on responds of the same section with moulded capitals, may reproduce the form of its medieval predecessor. A photograph of the church interior in 1856[16] shows a pointed arch of roughly the present dimensions, much plastered over and apparently with plain square jambs.

The priest's door on the south side of the chancel has a slightly pointed head with a simple continuous chamfer of head and jambs. This too could well be 13th century work.

THE 15th AND 16th CENTURIES

As well as the eastern extension of the chancel, several of the larger inserted windows in the church, and the interesting sedilia all look to be later medieval work.

In the south wall of the chancel are three two-light windows. The easternmost is totally Victorian, replacing a blocked square-headed window which may have been post-medieval[17]. The other two windows now have simple tracery of late 13th or early 14th century form. The tracery is all 19th century; a plan of the church in 1864[18] shows each window to have been a single broad light at this date. The somewhat distorted pointed rear arches appear to be genuine medieval work, but are not really dateable.

In the north wall of the chancel, near its west end, was a two-light window, moved in 1883 to the north end of the new organ chamber. This is probably of late 15th or early 16th century date, having two cinquefoil-headed lights under a flat pointed arch, with a broad hollow chamfer of head and jambs internally.

In the south wall of the nave is a late three-light window, with broad trefoil-headed lights with panel tracery over, under a square head. Several medieval cross slabs have been utilised in the construction of this window, which is probably of early 16th century date. The shape of the small cusped lights of the window head, the cusps almost meeting to divide off the circle at the head of the light, is seen again in the rood screen.

Internally, at the east end of the south wall of the chancel is an aumbry, now fitted with a door which conceals its stonework. West of this are the sedilia, which take the unusual form of a simple stone bench with shaped arms, all of stone. Similar benches occur at the two neighbouring churches of Campsall and Owston.

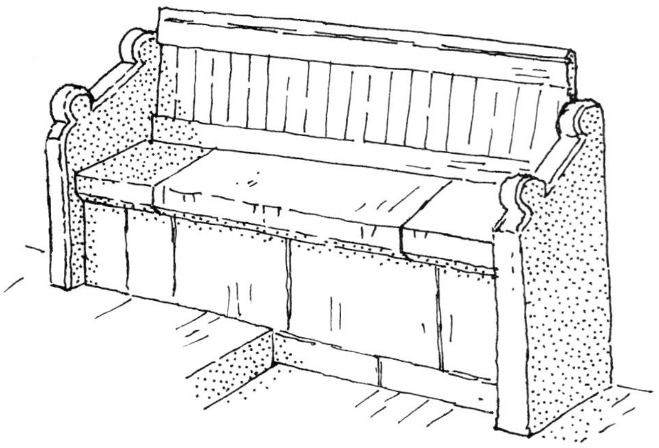

Stone Sedilia

The south porch appears to be a 14th or 15th century addition and is again of a distinctive local type, common on the Magnesian Limestone. The slab roof is carried on four chamfered arched ribs. The stone benches on either side are original, but the outer arch, of four-centred form with a continuous chamfer and a chamfered hoodmould with turned-back ends, is largely a restoration.

The embattled tower parapet, with its gargoyles and small crocketted pinnacles, is typical of the 15th century alterations to most of the church towers in the area.

POST-MEDIEVAL ALTERATIONS

As is usual in the area, Victorian restorers swept away most traces of post-Reformation alterations to the church, especially those made in what they termed the domestic style of the 17th and 18th centuries. Typical of this at Burghwallis was a two-light square-headed window in the south wall of the nave above the porch, which has now disappeared without trace.

A large buttress of considerable projection on the south side of the chancel, which may have been of 17th century construction (a similar buttress at Hooton Pagnell, which has been allowed to survive, is dated 1677) was replaced by a smaller and quite obviously 19th century successor.

In addition to the alterations to windows already referred to, the restorations of 1864 and 1883 were responsible for the construction of the organ chamber and the insertion of two two-light windows in the north wall of the nave, with a new buttress between them partly obscuring the blocked medieval north door.

The roof of the church and virtually all the stained glass of its windows also appear to be of Victorian date.

NON-STRUCTURAL FEATURES OF INTEREST

THE FONT

Situated in the south-west corner of the nave, this has a shallow circular bowl set upon an octagonal shaft. The bowl could be a 12th century piece, although the octagonal shaft suggests 14th or 15th century alteration. The lower part of the shaft and square plinth look Victorian.

THE ROOD SCREEN

The well preserved rood screen, restored by the rector in 1881, according to an attached plaque, is a good piece of late medieval work. There are six bays with ogee-headed openings and complex tracery above, the central pair over a segmental-headed arch. The coved canopy has a cornice with vine trails which looks largely restoration work. There is a very similar rood screen at Owston 1 mile (1.5 km.) to the south-east given by William Adam, lord of that manor. Here the central doors survive and bear his initials. Since William Adam obviously had connections with Burghwallis (he is buried a few feet from the Burghwallis screen) it seems likely that he was also the donor of this screen.

MEDIEVAL MONUMENTS

Burghwallis church has a good collection of medieval cross slabs, with three late inscribed examples being of particular interest. These comprise:-

(i) A slab now forming the internal sill of the three-light window on the south side of the nave. Open round-leaf bracelet head, with round-leaf shoots on cross shaft but no emblem. Mid 13th century.

(ii) A slab forming part of the floor of the 19th century vestry, formerly the organ chamber. The cross form is similar to (i) but with the emblems of a book on the left of the shaft and a chalice on the right, indicating the burial of a priest. Mid 13th century.

(iii) A slab now forming the southern half of the chancel step. Clustered cross head and sword on the right of shaft. c. 1250 - 1300.

(iv) A slab now forming the northern half of the chancel step with ivy leaf cross head. No emblem is visible but the right side of the slab is hidden by the base of the rood screen. This type of cross head, dateable to the first half of the 14th century, is a distinctive local form, seen in quite a number of churches on the Magnesian Limestone north and west of Doncaster.

(v) & (vi) Two fragments of an ivy leaf head, one built into the external face of the west wall of the nave south of the tower, the other into the external face of the east end of the chancel north of the east window.

(vii) Another ivy leaf slab now forming the east half of the external lintel of the three-light window on the south side of the nave.

(viii) The west half of the external lintel of the same window is formed by part of a slab bearing a chalice, and what looks like one terminal of an ivy leaf head.

(ix) Part of the internal west jamb of the same window is formed by a fragment of a cross slab showing the cross shaft and what may be a sword blade.

(x) A small fragment built into the internal east jamb of the westernmost window in the south wall of the chancel bears a small portion of design and the letter 'T' of a rim inscription. This may have been part of an incised effigy rather than a cross slab.

(xi) A complete cross slab floor stone to the south of the altar, with a rim inscription to Richard Lyndall, rector, who died in 1460. Jewelled cross with a book on the left and a chalice on the right.

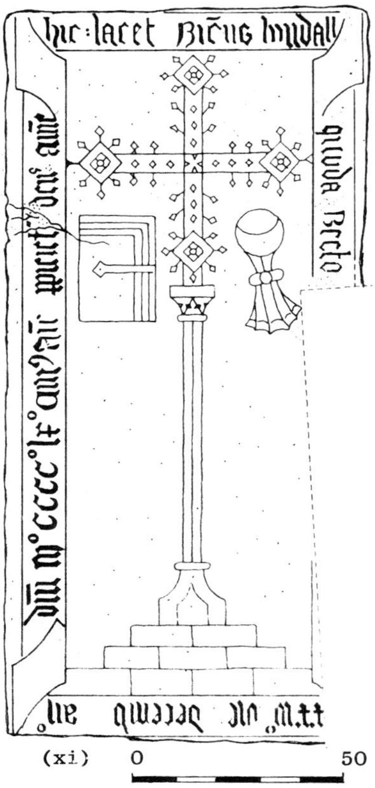

(xi) 0 50 cm

(xii) In the nave floor alongside the William Adam slab is a stone bearing a brass figure, c. 2 ft. 1 in. (0.6 m.) long, of a knight in plate armour. Although the accompanying inscription has been removed, this is generally thought to commemorate Thomas Gascoigne, who died in 1554[19].

(xiii) Complete cross slab floor stone north of the central aisle of the nave. The cross is almost identical to that of stone (xiv). The inscriptions on (xi) and (xiv) are in Latin, following the conventional formula, but that on (xiii) is a rhyming English one, difficult to interpret in parts:

Gētyl reder of your charite Pray
ye for me Syllm̄ Adā sūtym bale of this liberte
Now under this stone buryd here ask
that god who died for me siful mā
By his high mstie do not me try
But Adm̄ magna ... of my por sole he wold have mercie
the yer of our lorde MCCCCCliv and Ye ix day of april.

(xiv) A complete cross slab floor stone to the north of the altar. The cross is not jewelled, but otherwise almost identical in design to (xi), of which it is perhaps a copy. Rim inscription to Henry Gascoigne, rector, 1540. Coat of arms left of shaft and a chalice on the right.

(xiv) 0 50 cm

Altar

The pre-Reformation stone altar slab was found buried in the sanctuary during restoration work in the 1930's and restored to its original position.

REFERENCES

1. 1883 Elevation — Elevation with Faculty Ref. 1883/6, Borthwick Institute of Historical Research, York.
2. Taylor, H. M. — *Anglo-Saxon Architecture,* 111, 813, Cambridge University Press, 1978
3. Taylor, H. M. and Taylor, J. — *Anglo-Saxon Architecture,* I, 119, Cambridge University Press, 1965
4. 1883 Elevation — Op. cit.
5. G. Baldwin Brown — *The Arts in Early England, 2, Anglo-Saxon Architecture,* 245-246, London, 1925
6. Taylor, H. M. and Taylor, J. — Op. cit., 12-13
7. Taylor, H. M. — Op. cit., 948 & 964
8. Pevsner, N. — *The Buildings of England: Yorkshire, the West Riding,* 130. 2nd edn. Harmondsworth: Penguin 1967
9. Morris, J. E. — *The West Riding of Yorkshire* (Little Guide Series) 141. 2nd edn. London: Methuen & Co. 1923
10. Taylor, H. M. and Taylor, J. — Op. cit., 119
11. 1883 Elevation — Op. cit.

12 Taylor, H. M. and Taylor, J. — Op. cit., 119

13. Taylor, H. M. and Taylor, J. — Ibid.

14 1883 Elevation — Op. cit.

15 1883 Elevation — Ibid.

16 1856 Photograph — Photograph now hanging in church vestry

17 1883 Elevation — Op. cit.

18 1864 Plan — Plan with Faculty Ref. 1864/3, Borthwick Institute of Historical Research, York

19 Hunter, J. — *South Yorkshire,* 2, 486. Nicholls & Son, 1831

St. Peter's Church, Conisbrough

St. Peter's church at Conisbrough, although the subject of one of the most savage Victorian restorations in South Yorkshire, has some claim to be the most interesting ancient parish church in the county. It is quite probably the oldest church, embodying extensive remains of a Saxon minster church of probably 8th century date.

The pre-Conquest church appears to have consisted of nave with porticus to north and south, and perhaps flanking chambers to the east of the porticus, a chancel and western tower. In the later 12th century the Saxon building was remodelled, the porticus and lateral chambers being replaced by three-bay aisles. The 14th and 15th centuries saw the nave and the chancel extended eastward. Many ancient features were destroyed in the Victorian restoration, when the north aisle was rebuilt and an organ chamber added on the north side of the chancel.

In describing the fabric of this complex and interesting church, the pre-Conquest remains will be treated first, as a separate account.

THE SAXON BUILDING

The existence of substantial pre-Conquest remains in the fabric of Conisbrough church has been recognised only in recent years. Pevsner[1] drew attention to long and short work at the western angles of the nave, and one of the blocked openings above the north arcade has Saxon features. In 1969 Davies[2] described the nave and its early features in some detail, drawing attention to its similarities, both in dimensions and in architectural features, to the nave at Ledsham church (West Yorkshire) which the Taylors consider to be of 8th century date[3].

THE NAVE

The nave at Conisbrough measures internally c. 44 ft. 0 ins. (13.4 m.) by 17 ft. 4 ins. (5.28 m.); Ledsham is 46 ft. 0 ins. (14.0 m.) by 17 ft. 5 ins. (5.3 m.); with side walls 2 ft. 4 ins. (0.72 m.) in thickness. As Davies points out, the massive western quoins, well seen from the later aisles, are more correctly classed as side-alternate than long and short. The ends of the long stones of the north-east angle quoin can be seen from the north aisle, proving the nave to retain its original dimensions.

Above the inserted arcades remains of three original windows survive, their internal sills c. 13 ft. 9 ins. (4.2 m.) above the present floor level. The two windows on the north, above the eastern and western arches of the inserted arcade, retain their jambs and sills, the heads being destroyed when the clerestory windows were inserted in the 15th century. Only a section of the eastern internal jamb of one southern window survives. The height of these windows from the floor, their internal width 3 ft. 0 ins. (0.9 m.) and the use of alternating upright and long stones in their jambs (the long stones coursed in with the adjacent walling) are all very similar to the nave windows at Ledsham.

The dimensions of the external openings of these windows are difficult to ascertain, primarily because the amount of pointing which has been applied to the wall makes it difficult to

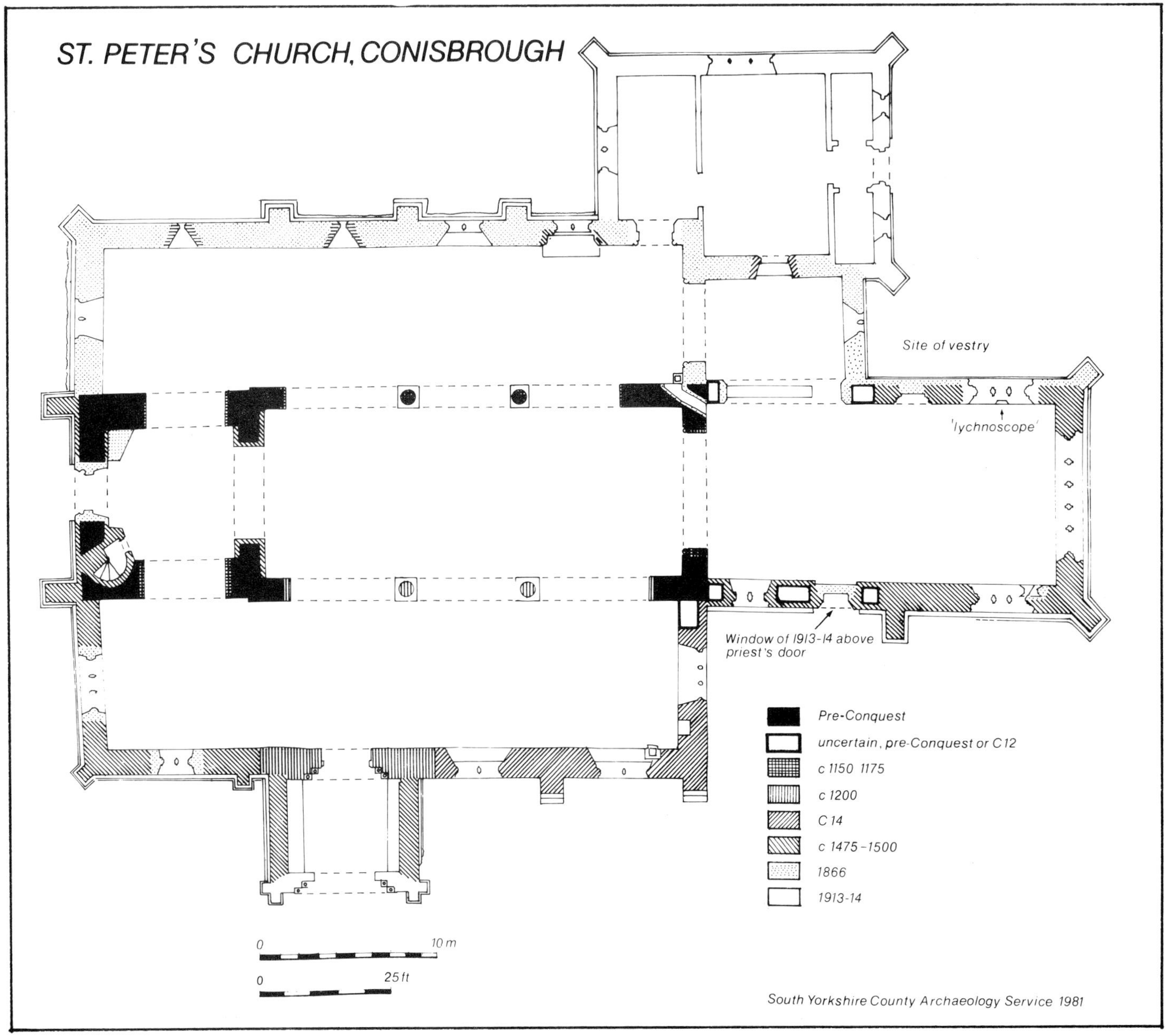
ST. PETER'S CHURCH, CONISBROUGH
Site of vestry
'lychnoscope'
Window of 1913-14 above priest's door
Pre-Conquest
uncertain, pre-Conquest or C12
c 1150 1175
c 1200
C 14
c 1475-1500
1866
1913-14
0
10 m
0
25 ft
South Yorkshire County Archaeology Service 1981

distinguish between the jointing of the masonry and structural features.

Between the two early windows in the north wall of the nave, and set rather lower in the wall, the head and upper jambs of a blocked round-headed opening survive. This is at first sight a very puzzling feature. On the internal face of the wall the opening is 1 ft. 7 ins. (0.49 m.) wide, chamfered all round, the head being cut from a single large block. Externally, the opening is 1 ft. 7 ins. (0.8 m.) in width, and the head cut from two large stones with a much smaller keystone between. Davies concludes that the opening appears to be an early Northumbrian type single-splay window built into the nave wall the wrong way round (that is splaying externally). He suggests that its function was to light a northernporticus from the nave, being set above a door from the nave into the porticus.

The splay of the opening does indeed suggest a window rather than a door, although at Ledsham the southern porticus (the walls of which survive as the side walls of the present south porch) was entered from the nave by an unusually tall doorway, the head of which was at a similar height c. 13 ft. 9 ins. (4.2 m.) above floor level. Tall and narrow doorways occur in several pre-Conquest churches, and it has been suggested that the reason for their height was to allow a processional cross to be carried through without its being lowered. Perhaps a more suitable parallel for the Conisbrough opening, again with Ledsham, would be the single-splayed window there which looks into the nave from the chamber above the west porch. This could imply that the porticus at Conisbrough was of two storeys.

High in the east wall of the nave, above the much restored Norman chancel arch, the sill and jambs of a blocked opening are visible. Whilst the masonry of the wall is of a similar character to that of the side walls of the nave, the jambs of the opening are not coursed in with the adjacent masonry in the manner of those of the early nave windows, the north jamb especially looking like an insertion. The south jamb has one 'long' stone coursed in with the wall, but its other stones look inserted. No feature remains by which this window or door can be dated. It may be secondary pre-Conquest work, or a medieval insertion. Medieval windows in this position are not common, although one does occur at St. Mary's church, Tickhill, only a few miles away.

THE NORTH PORTICUS

Apart from the doorway or window in the north wall of the nave, other evidence which has not been noted by previous workers survives for the existence and dimensions of the north porticus.

Perhaps the most interesting is that the lowest voussoirs of the arches springing from the eastern pier of the north arcade are cut so as to provide the springing of a third arch to the north of the pier, that is an arch across the line of the aisle. A plausible interpretation of this unusual feature might be that when the aisle was added in the 12th century, the east wall at least of the porticus was at first allowed to remain. If a lateral chamber existed east of the porticus (see below) this too might have been retained at first as part of the aisle, being incorporated into the new layout by having a Norman arch inserted into the wall between it and the porticus.

A ground plan of the church prior to the restoration[4] shows the north aisle to have a width of 10 ft. 2 ins. (3.1 m.), perhaps giving the length of the original porticus, if indeed it was incorporated into the 12th century aisle.

The north face of the nave wall, above the arcade, does show two areas of irregular masonry which may result from the patching over of the toothing of the porticus walls. These occur above the eastern pier of the arcade, and just to the east of the western pier, suggesting a porticus width of c. 8 ft. 2 ins. (2.5 m.) At Ledsham the surviving south porticus is simply built up against, not bonded into, the nave wall.

ST PETER'S CHURCH, CONISBROUGH

INTERNAL ELEVATION OF NORTH WALLS OF NAVE AND TOWER

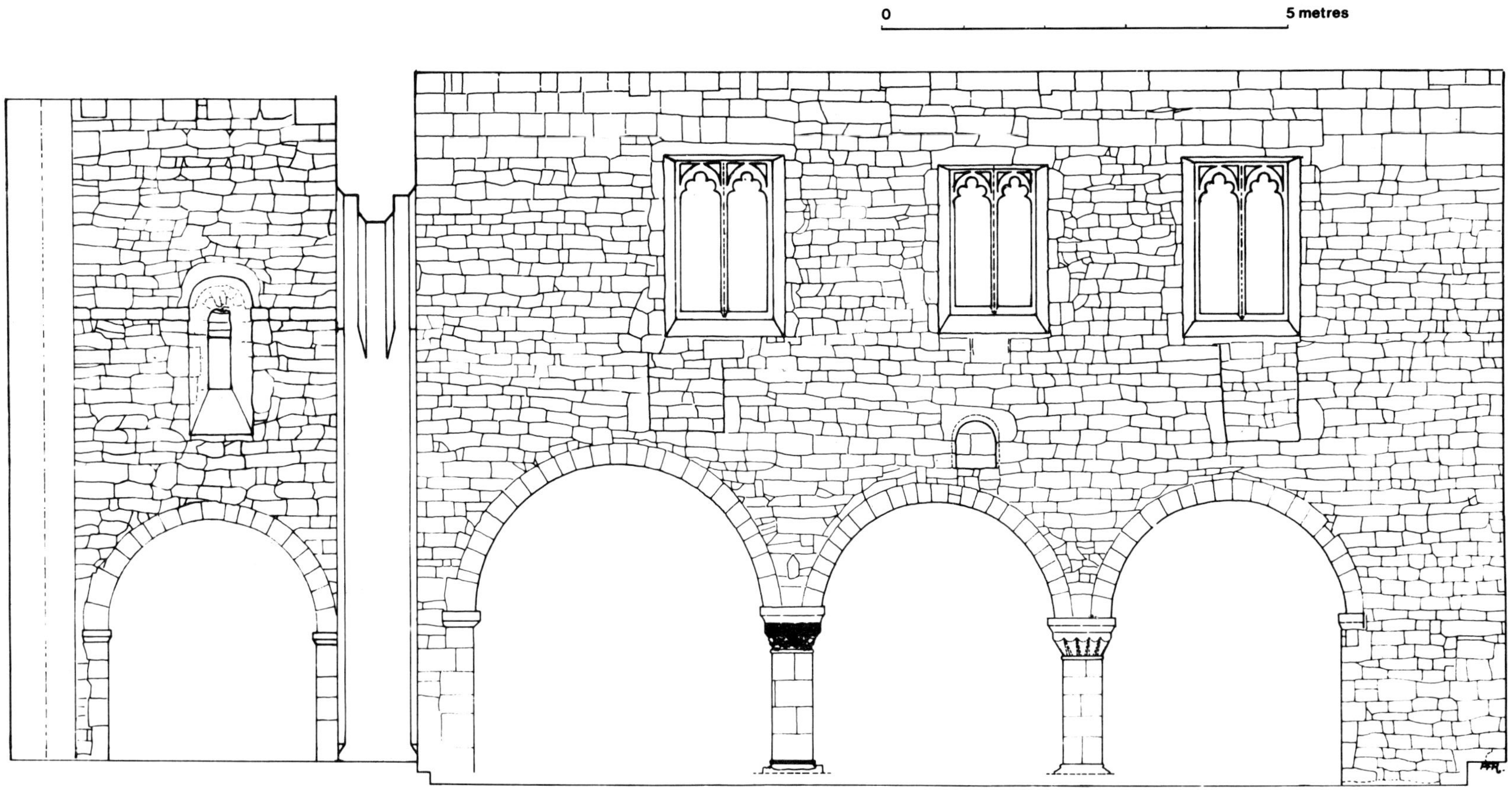

SOUTH YORKSHIRE COUNTY ARCHAEOLOGY SERVICE

ST PETER'S CHURCH, CONISBROUGH

INTERNAL ELEVATION OF SOUTH WALLS OF NAVE AND TOWER

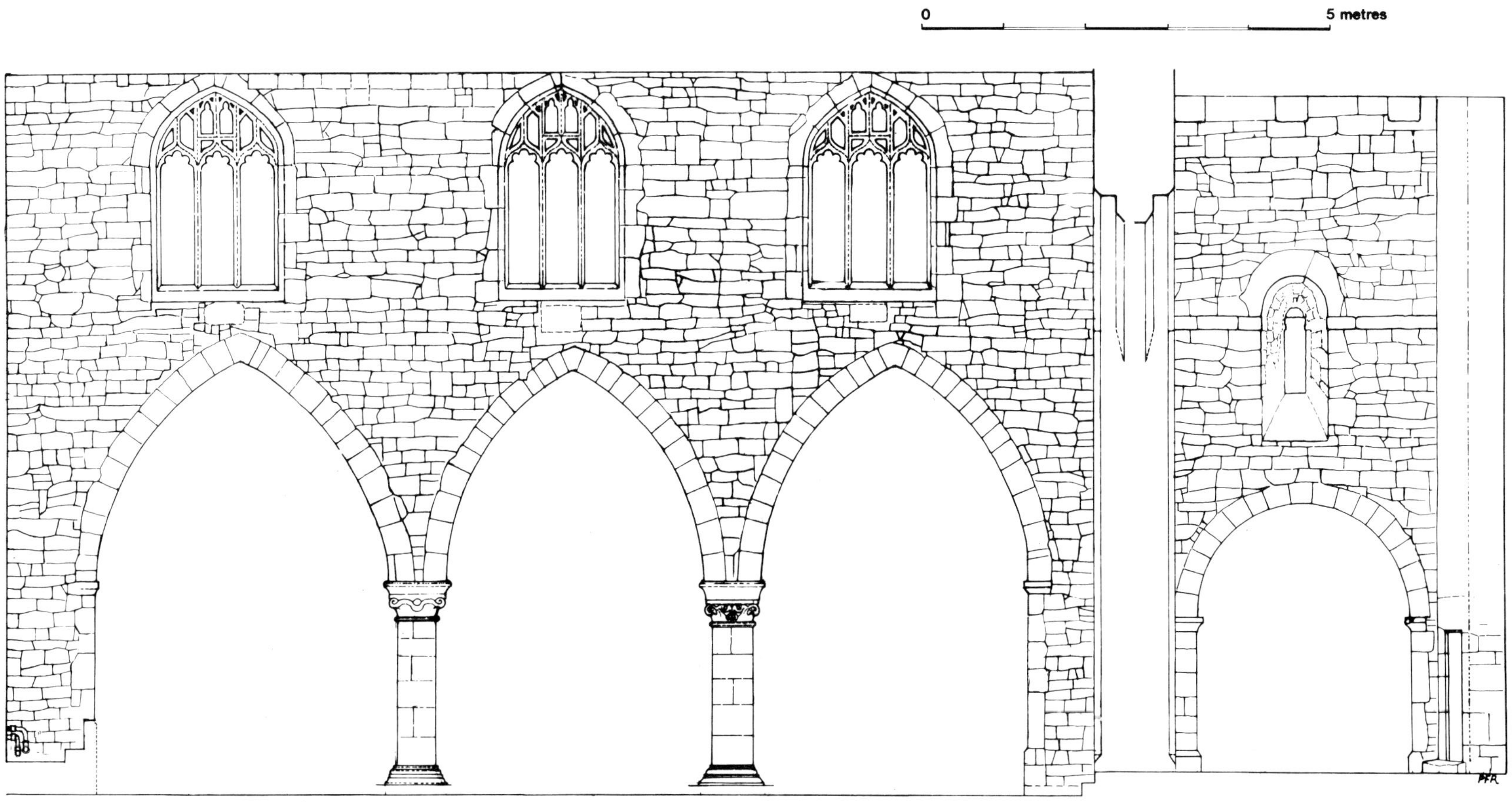

SOUTH YORKSHIRE COUNTY ARCHAEOLOGY SERVICE

THE SOUTH PORTICUS

The taller arches of the south arcade have removed rather more of the pre-Conquest wall than have their slightly earlier and lower counterparts on the north. The aisle itself, 14 ft. 9 ins. (4.5 m.) wide, is said to have been widened c. 1350[5]. A straight joint seen in the internal face of the south wall 5 ft. 4 ins. (1.63 m.) east of the door might conceivably mark the join between the late 12th century wall containing the door (if this in fact is *in situ*) and a 14th century rebuilding of the porticus wall to the east. This at first sight appears an attractive theory (compare Laughton-en-le-Morthen church) but would call for a porticus 14 ft. 9 ins. (4.5 m.) long by 8 ft. 2 ins. (2.5 m.) wide, proportions hard to find any parallel for.

EVIDENCE FOR FLANKING CHAMBERS EAST OF THE PORTICUS

Some slight evidence survives to suggest the former presence of chambers flanking the pre-Conquest nave to the east of the porticus.

On the north side of the nave, in the external face of the wall, a straight joint in the lowest four courses can be seen 2 ft. 0 ins. (0.6 m.) west of the south-east corner of the aisle. This may represent the east jamb of a doorway. An external doorway in this position is not a common feature in pre-Conquest churches.

In the internal face of the east wall of the south aisle, 3 ft. 0 ins. (0.9 m.) from its north end, are two upright stones which appear to have formed the north jamb of an opening, presumably a window. The upper part of this jamb has been cut back, probably when the present east window of the aisle (14th century work, much restored) was inserted.

A third possible pointer to the existence of chambers in the angle between nave wall and porticus is the evidence of the provision of (or at least the intention to provide) an arch across the north aisle springing from the eastern pier of the arcade (see under 'The North Porticus'). Rather than build a conventional aisle, the 12th century builders may have been happy to utilise both porticus and eastern chamber as part of the aisle, simply opening a large arch through the wall between them.

THE WEST TOWER

The west tower is generally regarded as a Norman addition to the church, heightened in the 15th century[6]. Externally, no feature of pre-15th century date is apparent, and internally the east wall (with the tall tower arch) and the west wall (with a doorway and window opening almost entirely 19th century in their present form) show nothing of prior date either. However, the north and south walls each have a plain 12th century semicircular arch opening into the aisle. Above these arches, and a little to the east of their centres, are windows now opening just under the aisle roofs.

The relationship between the tower and the west end of the nave is interesting. The tower has not been built up against the wall, but is in effect clasped by the nave quoins. The side walls of the tower are, however, not in bond with the nave. Both these features are paralleled at Kirk Hammerton in North Yorkshire[7], where, as in this case, neither gives any real evidence as to whether the tower is an addition or of one build with the nave.

These windows have round-headed rear arches, c. 6 ft. 3 ins. (1.9 m.) high by 2 ft. 5 ins. (0.75 m.) wide, and are single-splayed to outer openings 10 ft. 0 ins. (0.25 m.) wide and originally 3 ft. 3 ins. (1.0 m.) high. The heads of these have been blocked up. The rear arch of the northern window is cut from a single large stone, that of the southern from two stones. The jambs of the internal openings, unlike those of the early windows in the nave, are not

ST PETER'S CHURCH, CONISBROUGH

EXTERNAL ELEVATION OF NORTH WALLS OF NAVE AND TOWER

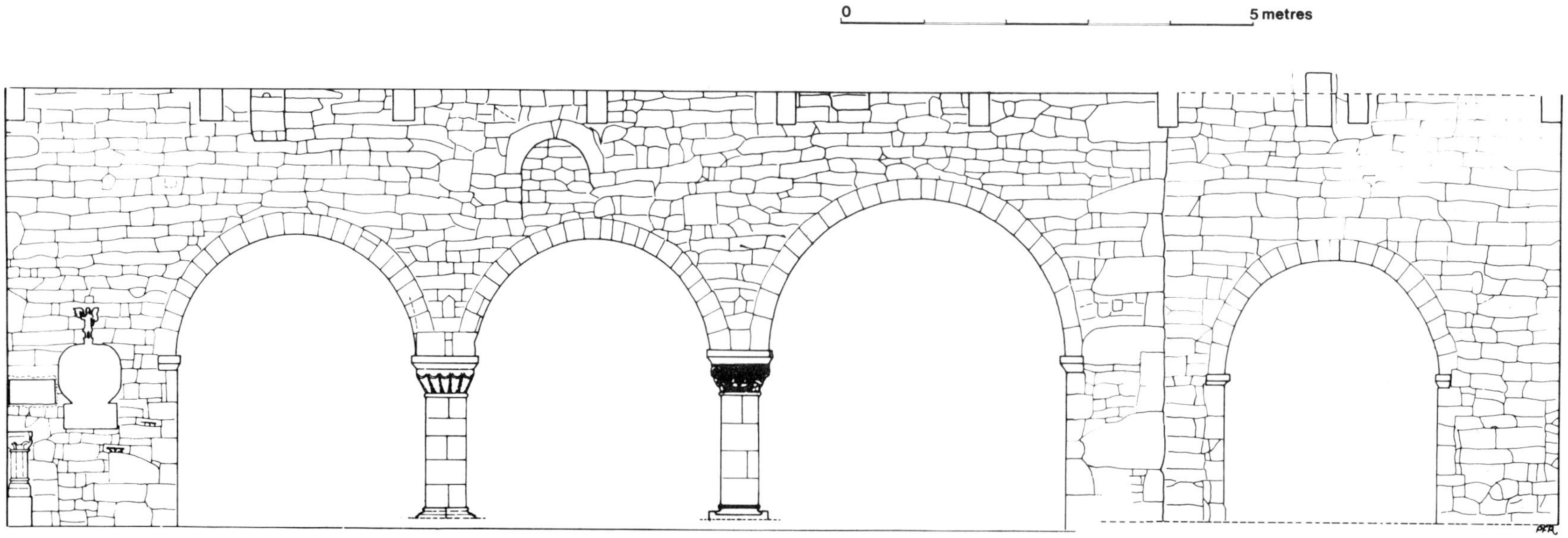

SOUTH YORKSHIRE COUNTY ARCHAEOLOGY SERVICE

coursed in with the adjacent masonry.

The rear arch of each window interrupts an internal string course of plain square section. This projects 2½ inches (0.06 m.) from the wall face below and 4 inches (0.1 m.) from the wall face above, producing in effect a set-back. The rough nature of the string makes a decorative function unlikely, and it may have served simply to carry a floor. Remains of an external string at the same level, running right up to the edge of the window opening, can be glimpsed through the southern window, although hidden from below by the aisle roof.

The nature of the jambs of these windows, and the manner in which they cut through the string courses, strongly suggests that they are insertions in earlier walls. They are themselves quite different in character from the 12th century work in the church, both in their monolithic rear arches, and in the generally crude nature of their jambs. They might be either Saxon or Overlap work. The walls in which they have been inserted are thus almost certainly pre-Conquest in date. The plain string courses, internal and external, would also suggest this. The internal string may have carried a wooden floor, or perhaps a roof plate, removed by the time the two windows were inserted.

It is unfortunate that the east and west walls of the tower have been completely re-cased, thus making it impossible to determine whether the original western structure was either a tower proper or a two-storied western porch such as existed at Ledsham. Assuming the lower part of the tower to be 8th century work coeval with the nave, the porch hypothesis would seem the more likely. The two windows may have been inserted in the 10th or 11th century when the porch may have been heightened into a tower.

THE CHANCEL

The present chancel consists of an almost square apartment lengthened eastwards in the 15th century. Evidence for the earlier phase can be seen in the change in masonry character apparent on the internal face of the north wall, and in the alignment of the squint from the south-east corner of the north aisle; onto an altar position little more than 10 ft. 0 ins. (3.0 m.) from the chancel arch.

The break between the 15th century masonry of the eastern half of the north wall (which contains many reddish stones) and the earlier work is irregular, starting at the blocked 15th century door and working upwards and westwards to what may be the jamb of a former window directly above the apex of the 19th century arch opening into the north chapel. A course of flat stones here, c. 3 ft. 3 ins. (1.0 m.) below the roof, may mark the upper limit of the earlier work, or perhaps a cut-back string course.

The date of this earlier walling, broadly similar in character to the pre-Conquest work in the nave, is problematical. The fact that the line of the north chancel wall is set slightly outside, that is north of, that of the nave, militates against this being contemporary with the nave. The original chancel would almost certainly have been narrower than the nave. Whether this section of wall is secondary pre-Conquest or 12th century work must remain an open question.

LATER MEDIEVAL ADDITIONS AND ALTERATIONS

THE 12th CENTURY REMODELLING

The remodelling of the church, supposed by Morris[8], to have been carried out by Hamelin Plantaganet builder of the castle keep, included the addition of aisles to the nave and the insertion of a new chancel arch.

The chancel arch, doubtless higher and wider than its pre-Conquest predecessor, is round-headed with a single roll moulding to both nave and chancel. The square jambs have attached shafts towards the nave with capitals of a simple scalloped type, bearing incised decoration which is probably Victorian. The impost blocks, chamfered below, bear an incised lozenge pattern on all three faces. The arch was retooled and otherwise interfered with in the 19th century and the outer band of voussoirs look to be of this date.

The north arcade consists of three semicircular arches each of a single square order, the western being somewhat wider and higher than the eastern pair. This suggests that the insertion of the arcade took place in two phases and is in itself further evidence for the survival of the porticus and eastern chamber, at least during the first phase of the remodelling. The insertion of the arcade, carried out by the arches actually being built into the wall before the masonry beneath was removed, occasioned very little disturbance to the Saxon wall above.

The eastern and western responds of the arcade are simple and square, with impost blocks chamfered beneath. The piers are circular with moulded bases, the western rather more elaborate, with some corner ornament, now much damaged. The capital of the eastern pier is of a typical Norman scalloped type: the abacus square and chamfered beneath. The western capital is a much more elaborate piece, with foliage and figures in high relief. How far this vigorous carving is a product of 19th century retooling is problematic. The Rev. J. G. Gibbs in a letter to the *Doncaster Gazette* dated July 16, 1867, defending some aspects of the 1866 work, claims "the pillars and doorway were recut some years ago, but the Restoration Committee is in no wise responsible for that"[9]. Some damage to the capital (the manner in which the faces of the figures are broken away) looks like the result of Puritan iconoclasm, and suggests that 19th century attentions were relatively minor.

The south arcade has three pointed arches, of a single square order with circular piers and square responds. Once again, the two capitals are quite different, the western again being the more elaborate of the two. This has a foliage design, with volutes at the corners. The eastern is simpler, of a typical waterleaf type. Each has a square abacus, hollow chamfered beneath. Both piers have moulded hold-water bases, the eastern with trefoiled leaves carved on the upper surface of each corner of the square plinth.

The arches by which the base of the tower opens onto the aisles are plain round-headed openings of a single square order, with imposts hollow chamfered beneath.

Stylistic evidence suggests that the 12th century remodelling took place in three phases. The chancel arch may be a little earlier than the arcades, Pevsner deciding that "it need not be later than the mid 12th century". He ascribes both arcades to c. 1175. However the pointed arches and more advanced capital and base forms seen in the south arcade might point to it being a little later than the north, perhaps c. 1200. The simple round-headed arches cut through the side walls of the Saxon tower imply that full length aisles engaging the tower were part of the reconstruction scheme from the first.

Little remains of the 12th century aisle walls. The north aisle, 9 ft. 10 ins. (3.1 m.) wide internally, was taken down and rebuilt in 1866. A plan of the church made prior to the restoration[10] shows a single Norman window near the west end of the north wall, and one is mentioned in Glynne's account of his visit to the church in 1853[11]. A second must have come to light when the wall was taken down, as two such windows, both apparently ancient, have been re-set in the north wall of the present aisle. An 1867 Sheffield pamphlet, decrying the restorations at Conisbrough and other local churches, makes mention of "the apparent paradox in the north aisle of very early windows in the heart of very late ones"[12]. Unfortunately no further explanation is given. The north aisle also contained a north door opposite that on the south, shown as walled up on the 1866 plan. Glynne refers to it as "... Early English ... with plain imposts".

At the south-east corner of the aisle is a pillar piscina having a square bowl with volutes at the angles, set upon an octagonal shaft. In its present form it appears 19th century, but is perhaps a copy of a late 12th century feature. Above the piscina is the rectangular opening of a squint, interfered with in the 19th century, cut through the wall to the north-west corner of the chancel.

The south aisle retains its original late 12th century south door, heavily restored. Whether or not this is *in situ* is uncertain. The door has a semicircular arch of three orders. The inner bears a simple chamfer continued unbroken to the ground. The second and third are carried on the crocketted capitals of (renewed) jamb shafts, and bear zig-zag and keeled mouldings respectively. The hoodmould carries typical Early English dog-tooth ornament.

The internal face of the south wall of the south aisle shows, 6 ft. 3 ins. (1.9 m.) west of the door, an irregular break in its masonry, with near the top of the wall part of the sill and west jamb of a window. Not enough survives to determine the form and date of this opening. The whiter masonry west of this point may be a 15th century rebuilding, although the situation is far from clear.

THE 13th AND 14th CENTURIES

Bearing in mind the markedly 'Transitional' style, making use of both Norman and Early English motifs, of the late 12th century south arcade and aisle, it is difficult to ascertain whether Glynne's 'Early English' north door was a 13th century insertion or contemporary with the wall in which it stood. Although no record survives of its removal, a medieval door which can hardly have come from anywhere else in the church is now set into the north wall of the 19th century organ chamber, and visible only from inside the 1913 vestry. This has chamfered jambs and moulded imposts, and a pointed arch of a single rather flattened roll moulding. There is a hoodmould of rounded section, terminating in circular stops each carved with a cross paté. These last are obviously 19th century work. This door would appear a late 13th or 14th century piece.

The outer arch of the south porch is a modern copy of an early 13th century feature, having a pointed arch, jamb shafts and a billet moulded hood. Its predecessor is described by Glynne as being an Early English arch, "with toothed mouldings and shafts with square abaci, much clogged with plaster". Since the side walls of the porch appear genuine 15th century work, this arch would appear to have been another re-used piece.

The eastern section of the south aisle appears to date from the first half of the 14th century. Its east window is of three lights, the central cinquefoil-headed and those flanking it trefoil-headed, with flowing tracery over, a design (unlike that of other restored windows in the church) quite compatible with medieval work. The tracery has been replaced, but much of the arch is ancient. The two two-light windows on the south side of the aisle are more of a problem. Each has two broad lights with shouldered arch lights, under a square head. This design, although uncommon, is found in 14th century work elsewhere, although more usually in doorway arches than in windows. The design is not one which a Victorian architect would be likely to introduce.

The east end of the south aisle evidently served as a chantry chapel, both piscina and aumbry surviving. The former, at the east end of the south wall, has a crude flat-pointed arch and a square projecting bowl, and the latter, a plain rectangular recess, is at the south end of the

east wall.
Pevsner considers the blocked door on the north side of the chancel, with its two continuous quadrant mouldings, a 14th century feature. From other evidence, however, the eastern part of the chancel appears a 15th century rather than a 13th century addition.

THE 15th CENTURY

The later 15th century saw a second major remodelling of the fabric of Conisbrough church, to give the overall Perpendicular appearance we see today. The chancel was extended eastward, with a chapel or vestry on the north, the nave walls were raised to accommodate a clerestory, and the western tower heightened. The aisle walls received new windows and crenellated parapets with pinnacles, and the south porch seems to have been rebuilt as well.
The chancel has suffered so much retooling and restoration in the 19th century that it is difficult to ascertain which features reproduce medieval work. Little old stonework is visible. The bold plinth of typical 15th century form, the diagonal buttress at the south-east corner and the stepped buttress east of the priest's door are probably original. The 1866 faculty[13] was "to repair and restore the windows ... as being of the same dimensions and character as at present", and it would seem that those at east and west ends of the south wall, and in the east gable, reproduce their earlier form. The east window is of five cinquefoil-headed lights with panel tracery over, under a somewhat flattened pointed arch. Jambs and head have, externally, a wide and deep hollow chamfer, also seen in the two old windows on the south of the chancel and the priest's door. Dodsworth, the 17th century antiquary, records the old glass in this window[14] as bearing a figure of Prior Atwell of Lewes, who entered that office in 1486.
At the east end of the south wall is a window of three cinquefoil-headed lights under a flat pointed arch. The priest's door has a head of similar form (a modern replacement) set on older jambs. At the west end of the wall is a 'low-side' window of two square-headed lights. Although its form and lack of cusping suggest post-medieval work, the hollow-chamfered jambs and head may indicate a 15th century date.
In the north wall opposite this window, a single-light opening is shown on the 1866 plan which may have been another 'low-side'. This was swept away at the restoration, no record of its form surviving. To the east of the modern arch which now pierces this wall is a blocked door, formerly giving access to the external chamber, probably a vestry. The jambs of this show a double quadrant moulding, continued round the flat-pointed head which is a modern replacement. Further east again and (like the door) visible only internally is the opening of a square squint or lychnoscope (as 19th century accounts term it) which gave a view of the altar from the vestry. A wooden door closing this opening was destroyed in 1866, but the old iron grille on its inner face survives. On the external face of the wall were a set of corbels (which probably carried a first floor to the vestry as at Sprotbrough), which did not survive the restoration. The east wall of the vestry, of which the foundations were laid bare in 1866, adjoined the north-east angle of the chancel, where the plinth was 'stopped' to receive it. This feature is now obscured by the 19th century diagonal buttress erected to match that at the south-east angle.
Internally, a moulded string course runs round the eastern half of the chancel at window sill level, on the north stepped up over the squint. This has been so heavily retooled that it is difficult to say whether it is a medieval feature or not. Equally difficult to date is the piscina beneath the string at the east end of the south wall, with a semicircular chamfered arch. The heightening of the nave walls to receive a clerestory (hardly necessary, as the pre-Conquest walls are unusually lofty) seems to have been coeval with the raising of the tower. On the south

St Peter's church, Conisbrough. Reconstructed impressions

The Saxon church, c.1000.

The church c.1200, after 12th century alterations.

the three clerestory windows are each of three lights, with cinquefoil-heads and panel tracery over, under four-centred arches. The northern clerestory is simpler, of three two-light windows, the lights cinquefoiled under a square head. The parapets of nave and aisles (embattled), and chancel, with their crocketted pinnacles, appear to be of the same date as the clerestory, although heavily restored. The 13th century nave roof survives, with some remnants of painted decoration on its eastern tie-beam.

The inserted Perpendicular style windows in the aisle walls remain of the same dimensions as those shown on the 1866 plan, but virtually all their stonework has been renewed. Their detail looks unlikely for genuine medieval work (in particular the west window of the south aisle, three trefoiled lights under a triangular arch should be noted). The two two-light windows in the north wall of the rebuilt north aisle, and that at its west end, are in the same relative positions as those of its predecessor, but here again their trefoil-headed lights under square heads look more like an 18th or early 19th century attempt at Gothic than genuine 15th century work. The eastern of the two windows has beneath its internal sill a tomb recess (in the same relative position before the rebuilding), with an ogee arch of two continuous wave mouldings.

The west tower, as remodelled and heightened towards the end of the 15th century, is an impressive member of a distinctive South Yorkshire group which includes Fishlake, Hatfield, Sprotbrough and Wadworth. Chamfered set-backs on north and south divide the tower into three stages, only the upper of the two being continued across the west wall. Two stepped buttresses on the west rise to just above the first set-back.

The lower stage of the tower opens onto the nave by a high four-centred arch of two chamfered orders, the outer continued down the jambs, the inner simply dying into the wall. On the west is a pointed doorway which appears entirely 19th century in its detail and masonry. Glynne describes its predecessor as of ogee form. The three-light window above the door is probably a more accurate copy of what was there before, the head stops and several stones of its hoodmould appearing ancient. Dodsworth records the glass in this window as bearing an inscription soliciting prayers for the souls of Edmund Fitzwilliam and Catherine his wife, which probably dated from the 1470's. A short pilaster rises from the apex of the hoodmould to carry the projecting sill of a canopied niche, now empty, which appears an authentic medieval feature. The niche has moulded jambs and a segmental head beneath an ogival pediment, which has been cut back and has lost much of its ornamentation.

Internally, the 15th century stair turret has been built into the south-west angle of the tower, entered through a narrow square-headed door.

The second stage of the tower has single-light windows to north and south, that on the north having a pediment above of similar form to that above the niche on the west. The south window has been similar but its pediment has been cut back to a mere fragment.

The belfry stage is well designed and impressive. In each wall are tall twin belfry openings, each of two lights and divided by a transom at mid-height. Above and below the transom the lights are cinquefoil-headed, those below being blocked up. The window heads share a continuous hoodmould, terminating to either side in head stops.

The parapet is embattled, with tall crocketted pinnacles at the angles and shorter ones midway between. Below the battlements is a decorative frieze of sunk cusped panels.

The belfry stage of the tower is very similar to that at Sprotbrough, the form of belfry openings and the frieze of sunk panels being almost identical. The Sprotbrough parapet is not however embattled. The Sprotbrough tower is known to have been 'of new construction' in 1474[15], and that at Conisbrough must be of very similar date. These similarities, and Dodsworth's record of

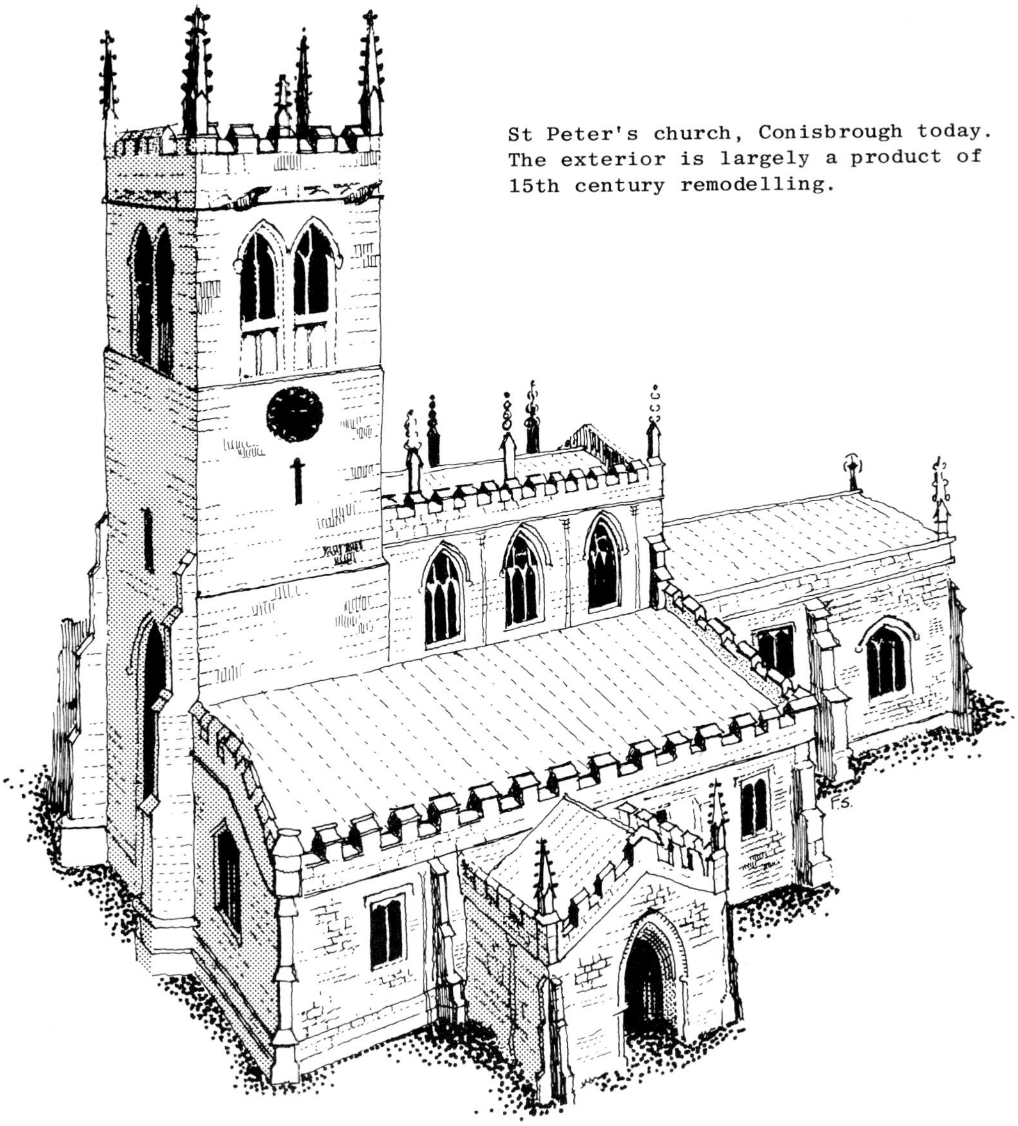

St Peter's church, Conisbrough today. The exterior is largely a product of 15th century remodelling.

the window glass, suggest that the Perpendicular remodelling at Conisbrough took place in the last quarter of the 15th century.

The Magnesian Limestone ashlar and parapet form of the side walls of the south porch are so similar to those of the clerestory and aisles that this too must be a 15th century rebuilding. The outer arch, if its modern replacement is an accurate copy, would seem to have been 13th century work re-used.

POST-MEDIEVAL ALTERATIONS

All evidence of 17th and 18th century alterations to the fabric was swept away in the 19th century. It would seem likely, both from parallels with other local churches, and from the spurious 19th century tracery in several of the aisle windows, that several of the windows had been converted into sashes. Most of the 1866 alterations have already been chronicled. The insertion of a block of masonry inside the north-west angle of the tower is also of this date. In 1913-1914 the present vestries were built, to the north of the 1866 organ chamber which is now a War Memorial Chapel.

NON-STRUCTURAL FEATURES OF INTEREST

THE FONT

The font is of 15th century date, probably coeval with the Perpendicular remodelling of the church. The bowl is octagonal, and set on a shafted stem. The west face of the bowl bears a figure of Christ seated, and the east a Resurrection. The remaining six faces have blank shields, set in quatrefoils.

MEDIEVAL GLASS

The only medieval glass surviving in the church is a jumble of fragments in the western window on the south side of the chancel (the 'low side'). These include the heads of an ecclesiastic and a female, variously conjectured to represent a bishop and a female saint[16] or Prior Atwell of Lewes and Our Lady of Dolours[17].

SAXON CROSS

Currently lying at the west end of the south aisle is a fragment of a pre-Conquest cross shaft, dated by Collingwood to the late 10th century[18].

MEDIEVAL MONUMENTS

(i) Pride of place among the medieval sepulchral monuments preserved in Conisbrough church must go to the elaborate Romanesque tomb-chest, now at the east end of the south aisle, dated by Butler[19] to c. 1140-1160. The coped lid bears a series of medallions enclosing mounted knights in combat, winged beasts and the signs of the zodiac. One side has a design of palmette leaves, the other a scene difficult to identify in which a warrior fights with an impressive dragon whilst a bishop with a crozier stands behind him. The warrior's shield is similar in form to that carved on one of the voussoirs of the south door at Hooton Pagnell (see p.).

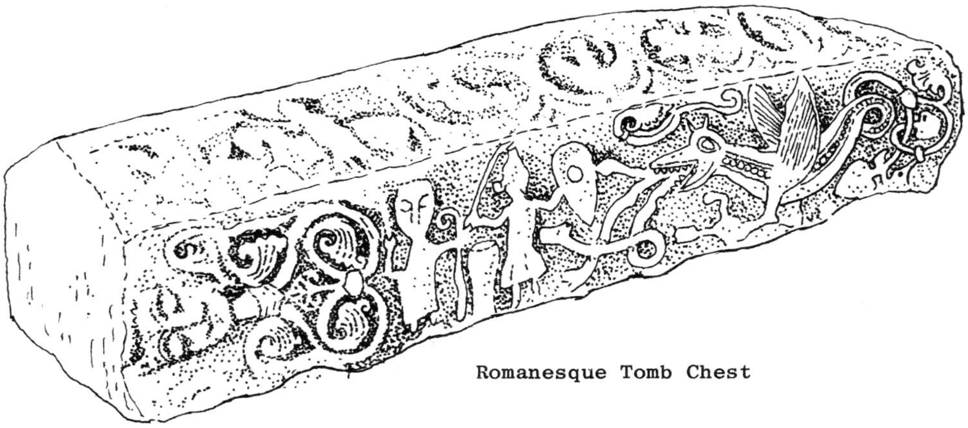

Romanesque Tomb Chest

(ii) Alongside the tomb chest is a tapering coffin lid bearing two birds (generally described as ravens) in high relief, much damaged, and a relief grid pattern on the chamfered edge of the stone at head and foot only. In the absence of local parallels, this stone is difficult to date.

(iii) In the north aisle is a medieval cross slab grave cover of a fairly conventional type, with a round-leaf cross head of early 13th century form, set in a sunken circle, with trefoil leaves and a motif difficult to decipher on the shaft beneath.

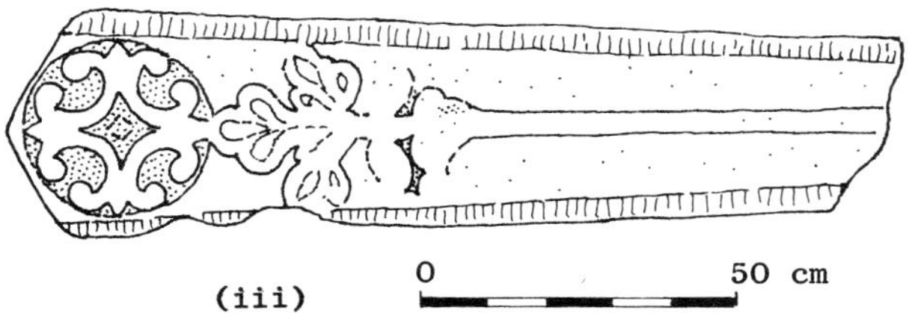

(iii)

(iv) The lower part of a second cross slab now lies in the churchyard just to the west of the south porch. This bears a deeply incised cross shaft ending in a point, with a ball just above. Perhaps of 12th century date.

(v) Built into the internal face of the east wall of the south porch is a 15th century slab bearing an inscription, weathered and difficult to read, in the form of a loosely coiled scroll.

(vi) A brass plate at the rear of the tomb recess in the north aisle bears an inscription commemorating Nicholas Bosvile, founder of the chantry here, who died in 1523.

(vii) Several medieval grave covers have been re-used as coping stones on the wall bounding the east side of the churchyard, but weathering has completely erased their designs.

<u>OTHER CARVED STONES</u>

(A) An interesting relief carving is now built into the internal face of the east wall of the south porch, above the 15th century grave slab. This appears to depict a woman, perhaps holding a child, seated on a couch beneath a shouldered arch. Although several authorities have described this as Norman work, the design has stylistic affinities closer to Romano-British carving.

(B) The external east jamb of the east window in the south wall of the south aisle incorporates a piece of 12th century carving, perhaps part of an elaborate grave cover, showing a running pattern of acanthus leaves, with pellets, in bold relief.

(C) Built into the external face of the east wall of the south aisle is a fragment of what appears to be a cross shaft, with a roll moulding at each angle.

(D) Low in the external face of the east wall of the south porch is a stone with a repeated motif of four lightly incised intersecting circles.

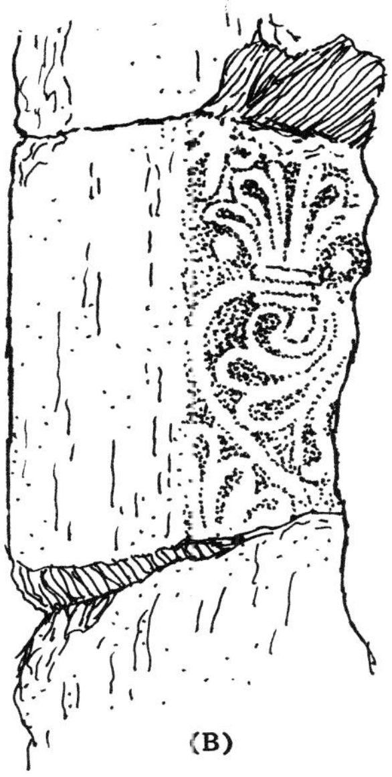

(B)

ALTAR SLAB

The medieval stone altar slab with the usual five consecration crosses and a niche for a small relic box, now in use in the War Memorial Chapel, was brought from the castle relatively recently.

FEATURES DESTROYED IN 1866

The pamphlet decrying the 1866 restoration refers to the destruction of a stone altar or table-tomb, 'ancient' benches and Jacobean woodwork, and various medieval wall paintings, some bearing inscriptions.

REFERENCES

1. Pevsner, N.	*The Buildings of England: Yorkshire, the West Riding.* 166-167. 2nd edn. Harmondsworth: Penguin 1967
2. Davies, G.	St. Peter's Church, Conisbrough, *Sprotborough in local history,* Pt. 2, Appendix III, i-iv, W. E. A. Local History Group, 1969
3. Taylor, H. M. and Taylor, J.	*Anglo-Saxon Architecture,* I, 378-384, Cambridge: University Press, 1965
4. 1866 Plan	Plan with Faculty Ref. 1866/2, Borthwick Institute of Historical Research, York
5. Cowen, B. and Braithwaite, G. F.	*Conisbrough.* (a short history to mark European Architectural Heritage Year, 1975)
6.	Ibid.
7. Morris, R.	Kirk Hammerton Church: The Tower and the Fabric, *Archaeological Journal* CXXXIII (1976), 95-103
8. Morris, J. E.	*The West Riding of Yorkshire* (Little Guide Series) 161. 2nd edn. London: Methuen & Co. 1923
9. 'Gaudens in Proelio'	*Church Restoration,* 8 - 9. Sheffield: Pawson & Brailsford, 1867
10. 1866 Plan	Op. cit.
11. Glynne, S.	Sir Stephen Glynne's Church Notes, *Yorkshire Archaeological Journal* XIV, 337-339, 1897
12. 'Gaudens in Proelio'	Op. cit. 10
13. 1866 Faculty	Faculty ref. 1866/2. Borthwick Institute of Historical Research, York
14. Dodsworth, R.	Yorkshire ChurchNotes 1619-1631, *Yorkshire Archaeological Society Record Series* XXXIV, 129, 1904
15. Hey, D.	*The Making of South Yorkshire,* 93-94, Moorland Publishers, 1979
16. Morris, J. E.	Op. cit. 10
17. Cowen, B. and Braithwaite, G. F.	Op. cit.
18. Collingwood, W. G.	*Northumbrian Crosses of the Pre-Norman Age,* 107 London: Faber and Gwyer, 1927
19. Butler, L. A. S.	Minor medieval monumental sculpture in the East Midlands, *Archaeological Journal.* CXXI, 126, 1965

All Saints' Church, Hooton Pagnell

The parish church of Hooton Pagnell, situated at the south end of the village and on the crest of the Magnesian Limestone escarpment, now consists of a west tower, nave and chancel, with an aisle (terminating eastwards in a vestry) running the full length of the north side of the building, and a south porch.

Rather more survives here of the early Norman church, with some Overlap features, than at neighbouring Brodsworth, where the church apparently originated as a building of very similar form. At Hooton Pagnell the church was enlarged in the late 12th or early 13th century by a lengthening of the chancel and the addition of a north aisle to the nave. The upper part of the tower was reconstructed in the 14th century and a chapel north of the chancel, with vestry, followed later, perhaps in the 15th century. Alterations made to the building in the 17th and 18th centuries, the replacement of earlier windows and the heightening of the nave to take a gallery, were mostly swept away in the 1876 restoration, when the walls of the north chapel and aisle were rebuilt.

THE EARLY CHURCH

The early Norman church at Hooton Pagnell consisted of a nave c. 29 ft. 6 ins. (9.0 m.) by 19 ft. 4 ins. (5.9 m.) internally, with walls 3 ft. 5 ins. (1.05 m.) to 3 ft. 7 ins. (1.1 m.) thick. The outer faces of the side walls are continuous with those of the west tower which measures 15 ft. 6 ins. (4.73 m.) by 18 ft. 6 ins. (5.64 m.) internally, its walls 3 ft. 9 ins. (1.15 m.) to 3 ft. 11 ins. (1.2 m.) in thickness. The original chancel, with walls 3 ft. 1 in. (0.95 m.) thick, measured c. 11 ft. 2 ins. (3.4 m.) by 15 ft. 9 ins. (4.8 m.) internally. It should be noted that the longitudinal measurement is given first in each case; thus both tower and chancel were wider than they were long. The walls of the early part of the church are of coursed rubble with occasional use of herringbone (that is a course set diagonally) as at Brodsworth. The angle quoins are of a simple side-alternate type. Externally, there is no division between nave and tower.

Architectural features of the early building to survive are the chancel arch and south door, and a vestige of a window in the south wall of the chancel. The tower arch has been generally referred to as an original feature, but there is structural evidence to show that it has been reconstructed at some date (see below).

The chancel arch is roughly semicircular in form, slightly 'stilted' on the south, 10 ft. 0 in. (3.05 m.) wide and c. 15 ft. 1 in. (4.6 m.) high. To the chancel the arch is of a single order left square, to the nave there is a single roll moulding and traces of a hoodmould which has been cut back flush with the face of the wall. The impost blocks have their inner faces ornamented with a series of incised lozenges, with a cable mould below. The imposts have been carried back along both faces of the wall, but like the hoodmould they have been cut back. Towards the chancel the jambs are left square, but to the nave the form of the roll moulding on the arch is continued as an attached shaft on each jamb, rising to a very simple bulbous capital with a ring

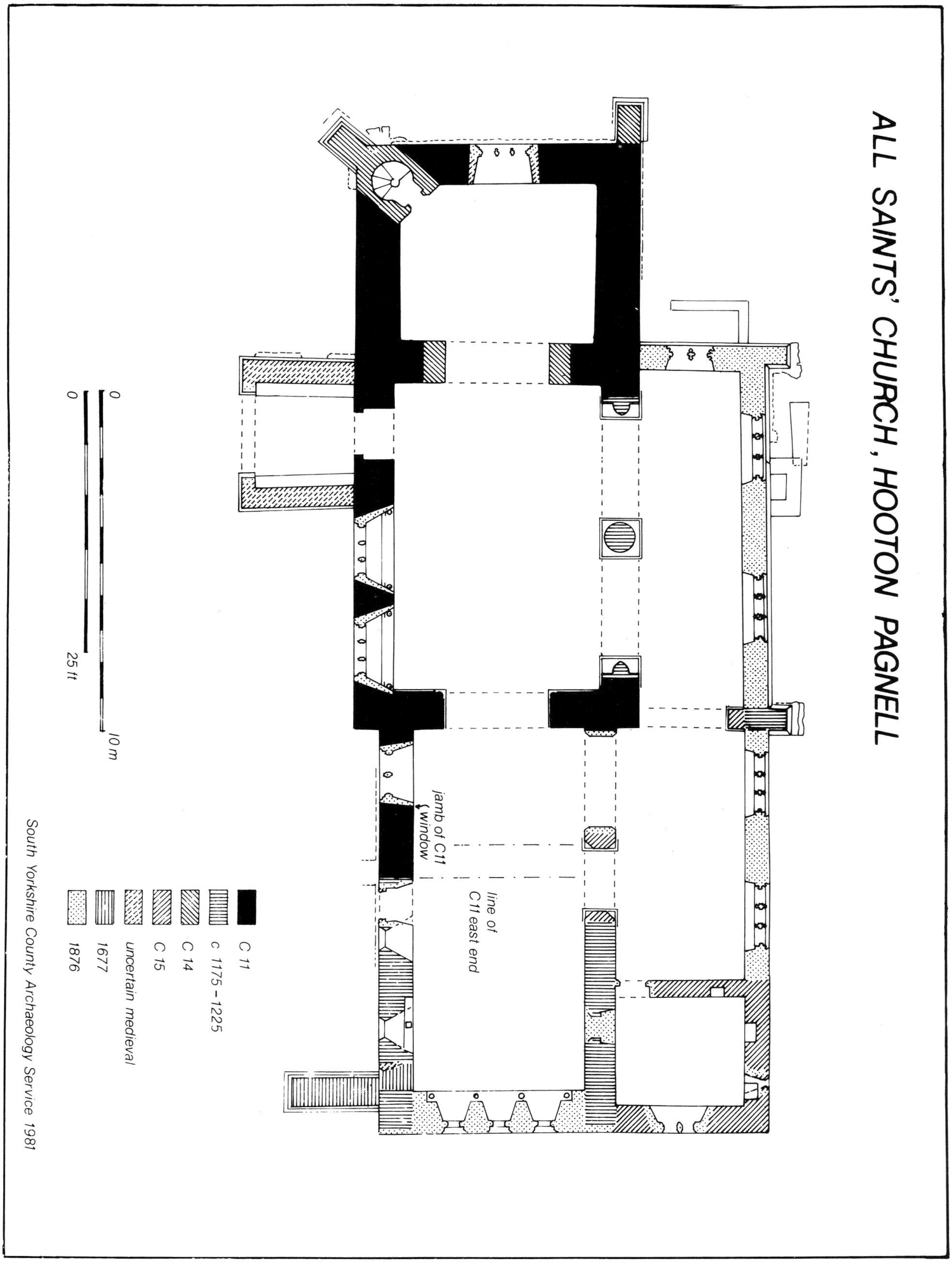
ALL SAINTS' CHURCH, HOOTON PAGNELL
jamb of C11 window
line of C11 east end
C 11
c 1175 – 1225
C 14
C 15
uncertain medieval
1677
1876
0
10 m
0
25 ft
South Yorkshire County Archaeology Service 1981

of cable moulding beneath it. The base is of similar section, with another cable-moulded ring. Some of the features of this arch show pre-Conquest influence. The capitals of the jamb shafts are quite unlike the usual Norman scallop capitals, and the incised lozenge pattern on the imposts echoes the design of the mysterious re-used frieze in the tower at Bolton-on-Dearne. The south door is a more typically Norman piece of work, a semicircular arch of one square order set on square jambs, the simple impost blocks being chamfered beneath and carried back along the wall to take the ends of a square-section hoodmould, beyond which they are broken away. The arch encloses a plain tympanum, the heavy lintel being original but the stones above 19th century replacements. The tympanum is slightly recessed above a chamfered set-back on the lintel stone. The door has two somewhat unusual features. Five of the voussoirs of the arch bear incised motifs. These are (numbering the voussoirs from left to right), (4) an arrow, (6) what may be a shield with a circular boss, (10) a dagger, (11) a key and (12) another arrow but with the

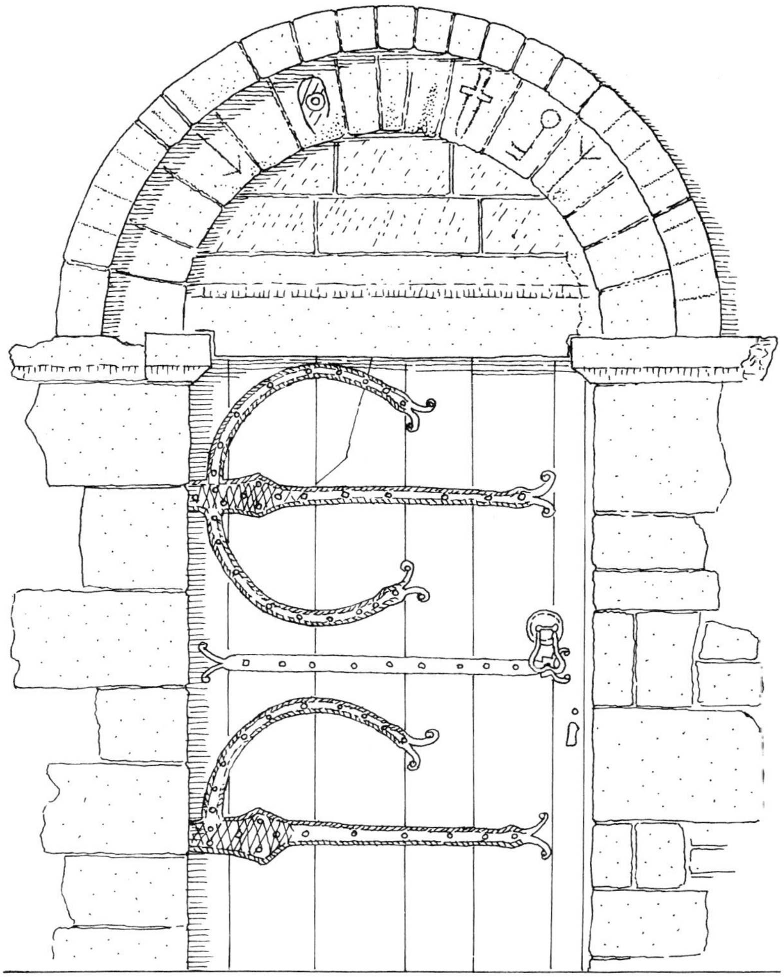

The South Door, showing early medieval ironwork.

0 1 m.

feathers shown rather than the point. Voussoirs (8) and (9) are badly weathered and may have once borne carving. No interpretation of these symbols has been offered. The dagger, or more commonly a full-length sword, and key are fairly common emblems of medieval cross slab grave covers.

The second unusual feature is the hoodmould. Six original stones remain, the nine smaller blocks at the head of the arch being 19th century repair. The larger original blocks bear a series of incised lines, as if to suggest a regular division between smaller voussoirs.

The chancel of the early church was extended eastwards in the late 12th or early 13th century. Both internally and externally the change in masonry type, from rubble to ashlar, is quite distinct, and externally a number of the original angle quoins survive. At the west end of the wall is a 19th century two-light window, the lights divided by a bifurcating mullion under a pointed head, in the usual 'low-side' position. A painting, now hanging in the vestry, of the church prior to the 1876 restoration shows what is apparently a medieval predecessor, probably of similar form. Internally, immediately east of the east jamb of this window can be seen a few stones of the east jamb and the first voussoirs of the head of an even earlier window, probably coeval with the wall.

The lower stage of the tower, from ground level to a set back at a height of c. 23 ft.0 in.(0.7 m), is obviously of the same build as the walls of the nave and early chancel. No original architectural features survive, however. The round-headed tower arch at first sight appears to be an authentic Norman piece, but a close inspection of it reveals several peculiarities.

The arch as it now stands is of three square orders to the nave and two to the tower, with plain square jambs and impost blocks chamfered beneath. The most apparent abnormality is the manner in which the wall is increased in thickness 12 ft. 4 ins. (3.75 m.) above floor level, from 3 ft. 11 ins. (1.2 m.) to c. 4 ft. 11 ins. (1.5 m.). This thickening is carried on a double chamfered off-set which runs across each face of the wall, and is carried on the outermost order of the arch on each side, that is, the third order on the east and the second on the west.

The voussoirs of the arch itself also merit attention. Those of the innermost order are mostly 19th century replacements, but those of the outer orders are of two quite distinct types; small stones with quite deep weathering, and larger blocks of a smoother texture, less weathered, the latter tending to be used towards the centre of the arch in each order. What this arrangement would suggest is that the weathered voussoirs are re-used from a smaller, narrower arch which has been taken down and rebuilt on a larger scale. This is further evidenced by distinct breaks in the masonry on each face of the wall 1 ft. 8 ins. (0.5 m.) to 3 ft. 3 ins. (1.0 m.) behind the jambs. The faces of the wall above the arch show none of the occasional use of herringbone seen in the other three walls of the tower.

Thus, although the tower arch is of conventional Norman form, it seems almost certain that it has been taken down and rebuilt, probably as part of the reconstruction of the tower in the 14th century. The upper two stages of the tower, of coursed ashlar, are entirely of this date. The belfry openings have two cinquefoil-headed lights with a quatrefoil piercing over, under a pointed head. On the inner faces of the north and south walls, at the top of the first stage, the wall face steps inwards and is carried on a double-chamfered course much in the manner of the thickening of the east wall 12 ft. 4 ins. (3.75 m.) above the floor. The buttresses at the western angles of the tower and the inserted newel stair at the south-west corner also belong to this reconstruction.

The original form of the upper part of the tower prior to the 14th century poses a problem. The early tower at Brodsworth, identical in ground plan to Hooton Pagnell, was replaced by a new tower further west in the late 12th century and its space thrown into the nave. At Darfield, 5 miles (8 km.) to the south-west, the more massive west tower has a lower part of early Norman rubble masonry, with later medieval upper stages. It hardly seems likely that in each of these three stages an early Norman belfry stage of stone was removed and replaced, simply for the sake of fashion or a higher tower. A more probable explanation might be that each tower originally supported a timber belfry (and spire?), which might be replaced in a more durable material within one or two centuries, either because of changing fashion or, more simply, because of decay.

LATER MEDIEVAL ENLARGEMENT

The chancel was extended eastwards, being more than doubled in length, in the late 12th or early 13th century. The extension is of ashlar, with an internal string course chamfered above and below, at the level of the sills of the two surviving lancet windows on the south. These lancets, towards the east end of the wall, were walled up prior to the 1876 restoration, when they were opened out. Most of the external stonework of the eastern lancet , the position of which was partly occupied by a sash window, is new, as are the flat-pointed rear arches of both windows. The priest's door, just east of the angle quoins of the early chancel, is wholly 19th century, replacing a simple square-headed opening of indeterminate date. Immediately to its west a projection of the rough base course of the wall may mark the site of a removed buttress. At the east end of the wall, visible externally immediately west of the large 17th century buttress, is a small pointed window perhaps of later medieval date.

Internally, the double sedilia beneath the eastern of the two lancets look like a poor restoration of an old feature. The heads of the two recesses are simple square-section arches, roughly semi-circular, the eastern a little higher than the western. The pillar between the recesses is a square block simply chamfered at the angles. Built into the rear of the recesses are a pair of 12th century cross slabs (see below). East of the sedilia is a cut away piscina bowl, but there is no evidence of the usual accompanying recess.

The east part of the north wall of the chancel appears internally to be relatively undisturbed 12th/13th century ashlar, without any features. However, some of this must be discreet 19th century refacing as the pre-1876 plan, now kept in the vestry, shows a door to the vestry here. The east end of the chancel with its three lancets is, despite Pevsner's ascription to the 13th century, completely work of 1876. The east window before this was a wide single-light opening described as "wretched" by Sir Stephen Glynne who visited the church in 1860[1].

The two bay north aisle of the nave is an addition dated by Pevsner[2] to 1175-1200, of which only the arcade now survives. The arches are pointed and of two orders, the inner chamfered and the outer square. The responds are keel-shaped with moulded capitals and bases, and the pillar heavy and circular with an octagonal abacus, the capital below having waterleaf ornament at the angles, plain towards the aisle but more elaborately carved towards the nave.

Prior to 1876 the aisle had a north door, described by Sir Stephen Glynne as "late, square-headed, labelled and of three lights without foils". The remains of the head of such a window, with flat-pointed heads to the lights and probably of 16th or early 17th century date, now border a gate-way in the churchyard wall south-east of the chancel. In 1876 the north wall of the aisle and perhaps the west end as well were rebuilt from ground level, with a two-light window to the west and two three-light windows on the north. The stepped buttresses at either end of the north wall probably survive from the medieval predecessor.

The next addition to the church appears to have been the chapel and vestry on the north side of the chancel. The chapel opens to the chancel with a round-headed arch of two chamfered orders on deeply chamfered responds, the chamfers rising from tall broach stops. Pevsner considers it "difficult to assign a date" to this arch, but examples of the use of such round-headed arches in the 15th century, especially where there was Norman work close to hand, are not uncommon. The north wall of the chapel is again a 19th century rebuild, in replacing a wall which also had two three-light windows (again 16th or 17th century insertions?) in similar positions. The chapel opens into the north aisle of the nave by a pointed arch of one chamfered order, with a segmental relieving arch over. This may be old work restored.

The vestry at the east end of the chapel has been considerably altered. The present door (at the east end of the chapel) and east window are of 1876. Above the east window is a blocked rectangular loop, suggesting that the vestry was once of two storeys, and in the north wall is a similar loop which appears old until the pre-restoration plan is consulted. This shows a wide sash window here. The restorers presumably moved this loop from elsewhere. Three square-headed cupboards or aumbries in the vestry walls, two on the north and one on the west, may be old. The more westerly of the two on the north has a drain running out through the wall.

The lower parts of the walls of the south porch, with their low benches partly composed of re-used medieval cross slabs, are probably medieval work but difficult to date. The outer arch, and upper parts of the walls are of 1876.

POST-MEDIEVAL ALTERATIONS

The windows in the north aisle and chapel, removed in 1876, appear to have been late medieval or post-medieval insertions in the medieval walls. Prior to the restoration, almost all the windows in the church appear to have been 17th or 18th century sashes. The south wall of the nave had a large two-light window, square-headed, to the east of the porch and a plain rectangular window above, as well as three smaller 'clerestory' lights in the upper section of the wall, heightened to accommodate a gallery. In 1876, when the nave walls were reduced to their original height, all these windows were removed, and replaced by two three-light windows of the 14th century style, to the east of the porch.

The three-light west window of the tower is also 19th century work, but appears to occupy an earlier opening; the internal jambs are old. An inscribed stone forming part of the internal north jamb, dated 1420, may give the date of the earlier window.

The church before the 19th century restoration, drawn from a painting now in the church

When the organ chamber was formed from the west part of the north chancel chapel, a large arch was broken through the west part of the north chancel wall, directly west of the medieval arch.

The large stepped buttress near the east end of the south wall of the chancel bears the incised date 1677.

NON-STRUCTURAL FEATURES OF INTEREST

WOODWORK

The earliest piece of woodwork in the church is without doubt the south door, with its 'C' type hinges. It has been suggested that both wood and ironwork are contemporary with the doorway, that is late 11th or early 12th century.

Two sections of a late medieval screen, with blank tracery of 15th or 16th century date, are now fixed to the jambs of the tower arch.

The pulpit is of 18th century date, with some good marquetry.

MEDIEVAL CROSS SLABS

Hooton Pagnell church is rich in medieval cross slab grave covers, at least eighteen surviving in whole or in part. The most interesting of these are:-

(i) A complete slab standing against the internal face of the west wall of the tower to the south of the west window. The design is carved in relief, and consists of a floriated cross with a complex 'clustered ring' head rising from a stepped base, a rectangular emblem (a book?) right of the shaft and a sword wound round with a sword-belt on the left. This slab is very similar to examples at Brodsworth and Campsall, and all may be the work of the same mason. 14th century date.

(ii) A slab standing against the internal face of the west wall of the tower north of the west window. A large and unusual slab bearing an incised Greek cross with spiral motifs springing from shaft and head. Difficult to date in the absence of local parallels, this is probably an early piece of work, of late 11th or 12th century date.

(i) (ii)

(iii) A late medieval cross slab floor stone, on the floor of the north chancel chapel. The design is mostly worn away, but traces of a floriated cross rising from a 'masonry' base are visible. Of the rim inscription only 'Hic iacet Joh...' is visible. Perhaps later 15th century in date.

(iv) A number of fragments of slabs now built into the internal walls of the south porch, of 12th to 14th century dates.

(v) A complete but very weathered slab lying in the churchyard c. 1 mile (0.6 km.) from the north wall of the north aisle. This may be *in situ*. Worn floriated cross, perhaps a 14th century type, rising from stepped base.

(vi) A complete slab, the upper of the pair built into the rear of the sedilia. Simple cross pate rising from a stepped base. What is unusual here is the very rare lower emblem, a notary's penner and inkhorn (another example occurs at Riccal in Humberside). The upper emblem is a book.

Another medieval monument, a plain slab with a marginal inscription, is set into the floor of the north chapel adjacent to cross slab (iii). This bears an inscription to William Stotfold d. 1507. The chapel was once known as the 'Stotfold Quire'.

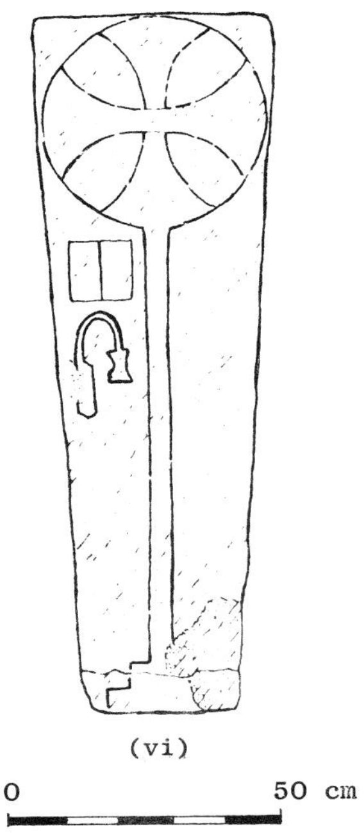

(vi)

REFERENCES

1. Glynne, S. Sir Stephen Glynne's Church Notes, *Yorkshire Archaeological Journal* XV, 498, 1899

2. Pevsner, N. *The Buildings of England: Yorkshire, the West Riding,* 267-268 2nd edn. Harmondsworth: Penguin 1967

All Saints' Church, Laughton-en-le-Morthen

The spectacular Perpendicular spire of Laughton church, set upon a hilltop on the Magnesian Limestone scarp, is a landmark visible from ten miles distance to north and west. The church, beside a Norman motte-and-bailey castle, has in its north door the best known and most spectacular piece of pre-Conquest architecture in South Yorkshire. The later medieval development of the church is complicated, and has aroused some controversy.

THE SAXON CHURCH

The reference in Domesday Book to Earl Edwin, an important landowner having his hall at Laughton, points to its pre-Conquest importance, and the standard of the Saxon workmanship seen in the church points to its having been an edifice of higher status than the usual village church.
The only unquestionably Saxon work to survive *in situ* at Laughton is limited to the west end of the north aisle, which incorporates the west and north walls of a pre-Conquest porticus 11 ft. 2 ins. (3.41 m.) wide internally (the toothing of its removed east wall can be seen internally). The walls of the porticus are c. 2 ft. 9 ins. (0.84 m.) in thickness, and constructed of coursed reddish-brown sandstone (the so-called 'Rotherham Red'). The north-east quoins survive, with three long and short pairs, of which only the northern face can be seen. The north-west quoin seems to have been removed in the 15th century, when the present buttress here was built. The Taylors' reference to the western face of this quoin being visible[1] is difficult to understand. Both north and west walls have a somewhat irregular double plinth, each part of square section.
The Saxon doorway has consisted of an arch 10 ft. 2 ins. (3.1 m.) high and c. 3 ft. 5 ins. (1.05 m.) wide, with a semicircular head and heavy square impost blocks. The voussoirs of the head carry a rebate, presumably as a decorative feature. The jambs of the door, and the lower inner angles of its impost blocks, were cut away in the 12th century to allow the insertion of a small doorway.
The Saxon door is cut straight through the wall, the voussoirs of its head appearing to be throughstones. The Taylors claim the inner jambs as original through their being coursed in with the adjacent walling, an observation which would seem open to question. The inner face of the doorhead bears a shallow rebate like the outer, but restricted to the seven inner voussoirs.
Externally, the door is outlined by bold stripwork, vertical pilasters rising to square block 'capitals' which rest on the top of the doorway imposts, from similar bases set on the upper plinth. The line of the pilasters is continued as a hoodmould around the doorhead, most of the stones of which are noticeably wider than the actual projection.
Lynam noted that the two lower stones of the arch on the east side are modern[2] and that "there has been a certain amount of restoration generally". This is not now apparent.
To the east of the eastern pilaster of the door, just below its 'capital', and in line with the impost, there is a stone flush with the face of the walling cut to an 'L' shape, as if to form the commencement of an outer hoodmould. That this is an intentional feature is borne out by a

ALL SAINTS CHURCH, LAUGHTON-EN-LE-MORTHEN

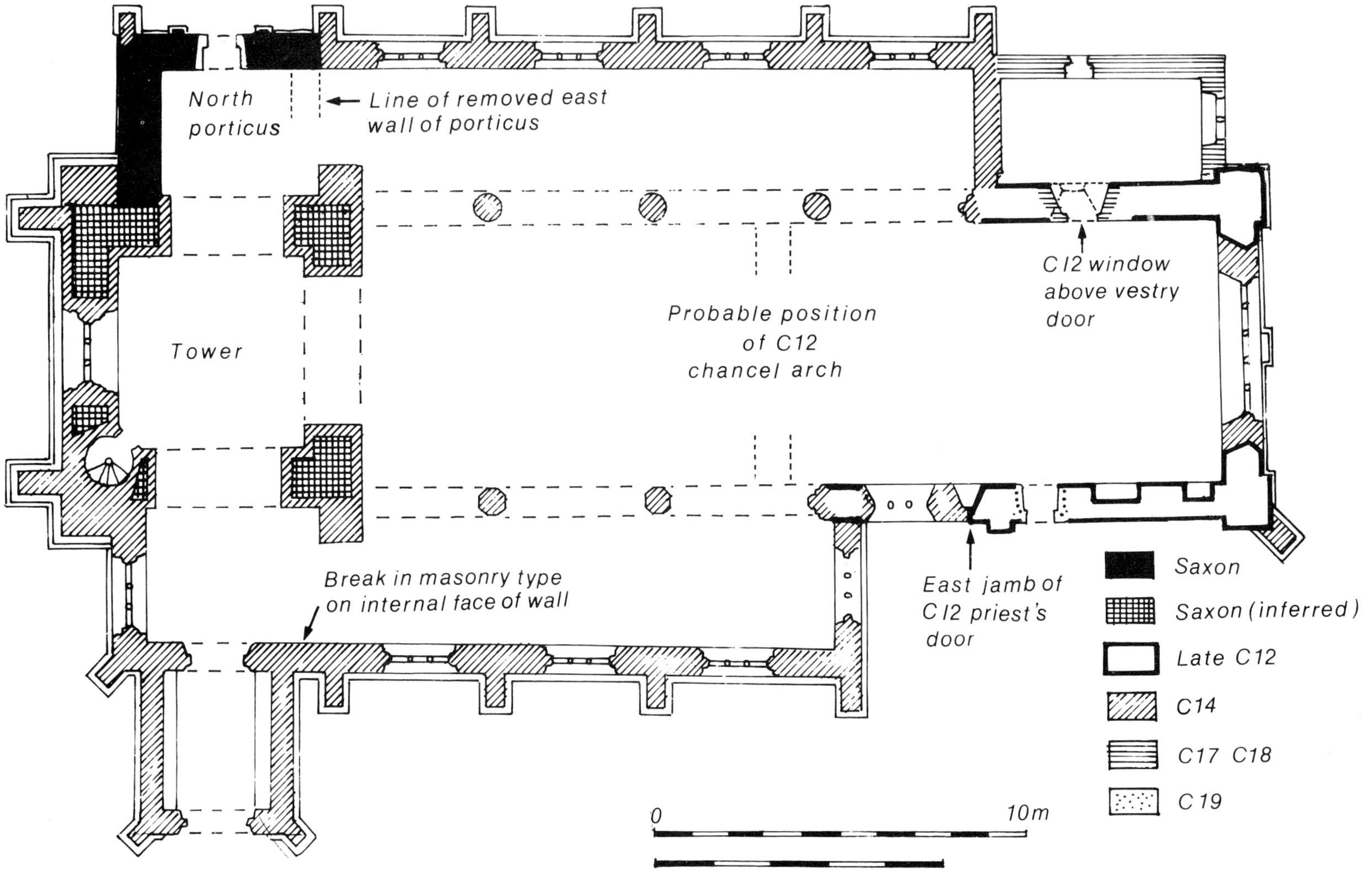

South Yorkshire County Archaeology Service 1981

stone of similar dimensions, although not so noticeably shaped, on the west. Whether this outer hoodmould or strip was ever actually constructed seems doubtful, although the masonry of the wall is so rough and irregular that subsequent disturbance might not be obvious.

The lower part of the chancel walls are of the same reddish sandstone as the porticus, and were considered by Rigby[3] to be Saxon work. The Taylors[4] consider the sandstone here a 12th century re-use of material from the earlier church, on the basis of a chamfered plinth of Norman form, although they leave open the question as to whether the two lower plinths of plain square section represent pre-Conquest work *in situ*. The gable-headed piscina at the east end of the south wall of the chancel is often claimed as Saxon on the basis of its form, but a close inspection suggests that it is put together from re-used material. The two slabs which form the triangular head are rebated for a door, but the jambs are not.

THE PLAN OF THE SAXON CHURCH

When all that remains *in situ* of the pre-Conquest fabric is one porticus, it is difficult, without excavation, to reconstruct the original plan of the remainder of the building. The Taylors[5] consider the porticus to have formed part of a complex of western chambers, such as is evidenced at Brixworth and Monkwearmouth, and date it to period 'C'.

To judge from the amount of re-used sandstone in the present fabric, the Saxon church must have been a building of considerable dimensions. Local quarries in the Magnesian Limestone were in use by the 12th century, as proved by the Norman ashlar and rubble stonework in the chancel. The late 14th century walls of aisles, porch and tower are all faced in limestone, yet all make heavy use internally of the red sandstone, which must originate from an earlier building since sandstone would not be imported from several miles away merely for this purpose.

The former presence of a southern counterpart to the surviving porticus is suggested by the discrepancy between the masonry of the internal face of the western bay of the south aisle wall (coursed blocks of red sandstone) and that of the remainder of the aisle wall further east (smaller courses of mixed sandstone and limestone). This does not imply the survival of pre-Conquest fabric *in situ* here, but two phases of later medieval building, as one might expect if a porticus had been allowed to survive whilst the eastern section of the aisle was constructed, before being replaced itself. This is very much the same situation as envisaged at Conisbrough. Unfortunately the joint between the two sections of walling here is obscured by the reparation of a 19th century flue. The external face of the wall is all of Magnesian Limestone ashlar.

If the present chancel is in fact built on pre-Conquest foundations, then the early church would have been of much the same length as at present, with the porticus, as the Taylors suggested, set north and south of its west end. However, a consideration of one feature of the ground plan of the present building, the relationship between the north porticus and the west tower, gives rise to an interesting alternative possibility. The porticus projects from the centre of the north side of the tower, which is noticeably broader than the porticus. This is precisely the relationship between the porticus and crossing of a number of Saxon churches (for example, Stow in Lincolnshire), where a broad square crossing, which would probably carry a wooden belfry rather than a stone tower, had narrower limbs on each side. It is an intriguing thought that the Laughton tower might be raised on a Saxon crossing of this type. No pre-Conquest fabric is now evident in the tower, except for re-used stone, the inner faces of the walls between the vault and belfry are almost entirely well-coursed red sandstone, but this would hardly be expected with the re-casing and strengthening of the walls necessary to carry such a high tower and spire.

If the west tower at Laughton does represent the crossings of the Saxon church, the fact that the Normans built their nave and chancel to the east of it rather than following the original layout might well be explicable by the presence of the motte-and-bailey castle. If one imagines the Norman builders coming to reconstruct a ruinous church in the second half of the 12th century, they might well have found its proximity to the earth-and-timber castle, which was probably constructed towards the end of the 11th century, inconvenient, as the castle ditch is only 60 ft. 0 in. (18.2 m.) from the west end of the present church. A partial solution to this problem would have been to retain the old crossing and porticus of the Saxon church and rebuild to the east of them, whilst demolishing what remained of the earlier nave. This is all conjecture; only excavation might reveal whether in fact the foundations of a pre-Conquest nave survive in the churchyard to the west of the tower.

It should perhaps be noted that some of the largest pre-Conquest churches, for example Sherborne Abbey (Dorset) did have a 'crossing' layout at the west end of the nave, consisting of a west tower with flanking chambers or porches (the *westwerk* of a number of early Continental churches). The fact that the surviving porticus at Laughton is somewhat unusual in having a large doorway in its end wall could suggest a function as a porch, most likely sited at or near the west end.

THE NORMAN RECONSTRUCTION

The church was remodelled and partly rebuilt in the second half of the 12th century, an aisled nave and a spacious chancel being provided, to the east of the Saxon porticus and tower. Nothing survives *in situ* of the 12th century nave. The generous proportions of the new chancel perhaps were intended to compensate for a less roomy nave in which pre-Conquest work might have been allowed to survive.

The Norman chancel, re-using red sandstone in its lower walls, was mostly constructed in Magnesian Limestone, ashlar for the north wall, the dressings around openings and the buttresses, and rubble for the south and east walls. Shallow pilaster buttresses were set at the eastern angles and midway along the side walls, and externally a string course, now mostly cut back flush with the wall, ran round the chancel at window sill level. The original internal length of the chancel was probably c. 37 ft. 1 in. (11.3 m.), with a chancel arch roughly in line with the centre of the eastern bay of the present nave (lengthened eastward in the 14th century remodelling).

The south wall of the chancel retains both its pilaster buttresses. Just to the west of the western buttress the east jamb of a blocked priest's door is visible externally, with one stone of the cut back hoodmould around its arched head. Inside, the east jamb and rather more of the head remain, utilised in the 14th century to form the east side of a lancet-shaped recess. Above the string course, to the east of the buttress, the west jamb and part of the head of a 12th century window survive, with a hoodmould which is now cut back both internally and externally. East of this is a later medieval window with, immediately to the east of its east jamb, a single upright stone of the eastern jamb of a former opening. Rather more of this jamb can be seen internally in several upright stones and only one horizontal one coursed in with the adjacent wall. Although the stone used is of the same type as in the 12th century chancel windows, the technique of jamb construction is quite different. As nothing remains of the head, sill or west jamb of this opening its form and date must remain a mystery.

Internally, at the east end of the south wall are a piscina and sedile. The gable-headed piscina has already been referred to as re-using earlier material. Its bowl is 19th century. The sedile is a simple round-arched recess with a continuous chamfer of head and jambs. Its form would suggest a 12th century date but it appears to be an insertion in the wall.

The east gable of the chancel has a pilaster buttress at each end and in the centre a third smaller one, doubtless cut down when the present five-light window was inserted. The original fenestration of the gable has been a triplet of round-headed lights, - the outer jambs of the northern and southern are visible externally, and the outer jambs and part of their heads internally.

The north chancel wall like the south had a central pilaster buttress, of which only the upper part survives (visible above the vestry roof, in the angle between the chancel wall and the east wall of the later north aisle). To the east of this a Norman window survives intact, except that its lower part is walled up internally. West of the buttress has been a second similar window, of which only a vestige (the end of its cut-back hoodmould) survives on the internal face of the wall, just above the eastern arch of the arcade. This is the evidence that the north arcade, despite its 12th century columns, cannot be Norman work coeval with the chancel.

Most authorities regard the columns of the north arcade as being *in situ* evidence that the Norman church had a four-bay north aisle, but the evidence of the destroyed window noted above, along with the positioning of the pilaster buttresses, suggests that the 12th century chancel extended further west to a chancel arch. This was very much the norm in 12th century churches in this area.

THE 14th CENTURY REMODELLING

A second major remodelling of the church took place towards the end of the 14th century, giving the building its present largely Perpendicular appearance. Rigby[6] suggested that the church had lain in ruins for half a century prior to this, following the insurrection of the barons in 1322 when the inhabitants of Laughton petitioned Parliament to the effect that John de Mowbray and others had "despoiled" their church. Whether this actually amounted to leaving the building in ruins, and if it did whether an important parish church would be allowed to remain in this state for fifty years, seems open to question. However, the middle decades of the 14th century were not conducive to church repair and restoration.

Local tradition, cited by Rigby[7], ascribes the 'building' of Laughton church to William of Wykeham, who was appointed prebend of Laughton at York Minster in 1363, and who is known to have been one of the great church builders of his age. Certainly an ambitious scheme of reconstruction was embarked upon, the nave and aisles being completely rebuilt and the magnificent west tower and spire, soaring to 187 ft. 0 in. (57.0 m.), being raised. The interior of the church, in the new Perpendicular fashion, was open from west to east without a chancel arch. The initial scheme may well have been to rebuild the entire church. There is some evidence that the survival of parts of the Saxon and Norman fabric, and the re-use of earlier material, may be due to a modification of the builder's plan, perhaps occasioned by a lack of finance.

The new south arcade is of three bays, the octagonal columns having moulded capitals and bases, and carrying pointed arches of two orders, the inner chamfered and the outer with a wave-moulding. At the east end of the arcade the outer order is continued to the ground whilst the inner rests on a semi-octagonal shaft with a moulded capital. To both nave and aisle there is a wave-moulded hoodmould terminated above the shafts and eastern respond in elaborately carved busts of angels. The western bay of the arcade shows the first evidence of the frustration of the original plan for a total rebuilding. The arch is noticeably narrower than the other two, and there is no western respond, the orders simply dying into the tower wall, an anomaly repeated in the north arcade. A plausible explanation of this would be to assume that the builder's initial intention was to sweep away the earlier crossing/tower and erect a four bay nave, its west end in line with

LAUGHTON EN LE MORTHEN
The Pre-Conquest North Door

South Yorkshire County Archaeology Service 1981

the present west walls of the aisles. This would allow for arcade arches of c. 14 ft. 4 ins. (4.36 m.). In fact, only the eastern two, three on the north where the arcade extends a bay further east, were built to this span, whereupon a change in plan meant that the earlier crossing/tower was retained, and both arcades finished off with a short 10 ft. 10 ins. (3.3 m.) bay, there being no room for a proper respond.

Consideration of the four bay north arcade raises the problem of three circular piers with capitals of late 12th century form which Pevsner[8] dates to c. 1190. The three capitals are all quite different in form, the western swelling to a simple block, the central multi-scalloped and the eastern with a leaf at each corner, those to the north curling into simple volutes. The abaci have been re-cut with square flower ornament alternating with grotesque masks. The piers themselves are unusually tall for Norman work, 9 ft. 10 ins. (3.0 m.) from the top of base to foot of capital; compare this with the north and south arcades at Conisbrough with piers of 4 ft. 3 ins. (1.3 m.) and 5 ft. 7 ins. (1.7 m.) respectively. The pier bases are simple and rather crude although 'holdwater' mouldings might have been expected at this period. There seems no doubt that the piers and capitals are in fact re-used from the Norman nave. The space available between chancel and the crossing/tower would have allowed arcades of no more than three bays. The late 14th century builders would then have had four Norman piers available to them. The unusual height of the three circular piers they used in their new arcade is probably due to the fourth Norman column being cut up to heighten those re-used.

The eastern respond of the north arcade is a puzzling piece, consisting of a triplet of shafts with moulded capitals and bases, and square-section fillets in the angles between the shafts and on the face of the central shaft. Pevsner[9] ascribes an early 14th century date, so this is presumably another re-used piece.

The arcade itself has pointed arches of very similar form to those on the south, except that the stops to the hoodmould are now full-length angels, and below the point at which the western arch dies into the tower wall is a panel with a fine relief carving of a seated angel holding a scroll.

The aisle walls are of Magnesian Limestone ashlar, except of course for the sandstone of the surviving Saxon porticus at the west end of the north aisle. The side walls have a three light window in each bay and stepped buttresses between which rise to a prominent string course bearing the usual wave-moulding, visually dividing the wall into a series of panels. The windows have trefoiled ogee heads to their lights beneath square heads, the hoodmoulds above having well carved head stops representing kings and queens to the south, and spectacular full figure stops on the north. Pevsner[10] describes these as representing a lion and a bird, a knight and something unrecognisable, a king and a queen, and an angel and a devil. The western bay of the south aisle wall is occupied by the south door. Despite being covered by the apparently contemporary south porch, the door arch is very badly weathered. This is sad since it must originally have been a rather fine composition. The arch is pointed, with a hoodmould rising to a crocketted pinnacle. the jambs have a broad hollow chamfer and on its inner edge an attached shaft with a moulded base. The capitals of these shafts, and the arch mouldings, are completely decayed. The attached round shafts here, and the several appearances of the ogee form throughout the church show that the Perpendicular work here is earlier than the usual Perpendicular of the area, retaining several Decorated motifs.

The south aisle has a west window of three lights with elementary panel tracery over, and an east window which is a rather more impressive composition with three cinquefoil-headed lights and reticulated tracery over under a four-centred head. At the east end of the internal face of the south wall of the aisle is a piscina which, like that in the chancel, appears to be put together from old materials. The moulded jambs and bowl look genuine medieval work but the round-headed arch is 19th century work and the rear of the recess is formed by a slab containing the bowl of another piscina, set upright in the wall.

The south porch has diagonal buttresses at its southern angles and an outer arch of two continuous hollow-chamfered orders, and a hollow-chamfered hood carried back along the wall face on either side as a string course.

The late 15th century remodelling of the chancel involved, apart from the truncation of its west end, the heightening of its walls to a uniform level with those of the nave, the replacement of 12th century windows by larger Perpendicular openings on the south and east, and the addition of a diagonal buttress to the south-east angle. It was probably the intention to plaster or render the walls externally as well as internally, to judge from the deliberate cutting back of the Norman string course and the hoodmoulds of the earlier openings.

The new east window is a fine composition of five lights with subarcuated reticulate tracery above. The more westerly of the two windows on the south is really a 'low-side', its sill only c. 3 ft. 3 ins. (1.0 m.) from ground level. The three ogee-headed trefoiled lights have super-mullioned tracery over with the same cusped mouchette form seen in the aisle windows. The insertion of this window necessitated the destruction of the 12th century priest's door, a replacement for which was sited east of the pilaster buttress. The form of this replacement is uncertain. Hunter[11] shows a plain square-headed opening which has since been succeeded by a pointed arch which Pevsner[12] dates to the 13th century but which is very obviously Victorian. Further east is a second inserted window of similar form, with three cinquefoil-headed lights under a four-centred arch. This may be a little later in date than the remodelling, perhaps in the 15th century.

The west tower and spire are undoubtedly Laughton's most notable architectural feature, in their dimensions almost out of proportion with the rest of the church. Although the raising of the tower on an earlier substructure appears, as has been shown,to have been a change of plan, no expense seems to have been spared in the execution of the tower design itself.

The tower walls rise sheer externally to a set-back at the base of the belfry, with pairs of stepped buttresses at each angle and a tall moulded plinth. The lower stage has a west window of three lights with a transom, the lights having cinquefoiled heads above and below. The arch to the nave is pointed and of two chamfered orders, the inner carried on moulded corbels and the outer continuous to floor level. The arches to the aisles are of similar form except that the inner order simply dies into the jambs. In the south-west angle is a small door to the newel stair, which is lit by plain rectangular loops. The lower stage has a fine vault with longitudinal and transverse ridge ribs, diagonal ribs, tiercerons and a central circular opening for the bell ropes. There are bosses carved with foliage where the tiercerons join the ridge ribs. Above the vault is a single lofty chamber rising to belfry floor level, lit by a rectangular loop in each wall. The internal faces of the wall are all red sandstone, except for the inner face of the newel stair which is red sandstone for a few courses above the door into the chamber and then Magnesian Limestone.

The transition from tower to spire at Laughton is achieved in an original manner, more successfully so than at other spired churches in the area. At the base of the belfry stage the angles of the tower start to cant back, so that by parapet level the tower is a regular octagon, leaving only a narrow walk between the crenellated parapet and the spire. Meanwhile, the angle buttresses join to form diagonal buttresses which rise above parapet level as pinnacles, linked to the spire as flying buttresses, from which further more slender pinnacles rise alongside the spire, to which

All Saint's church, Laughton-en-le-Morthen

The church c. 1200, after Norman
remodelling of a Saxon structure

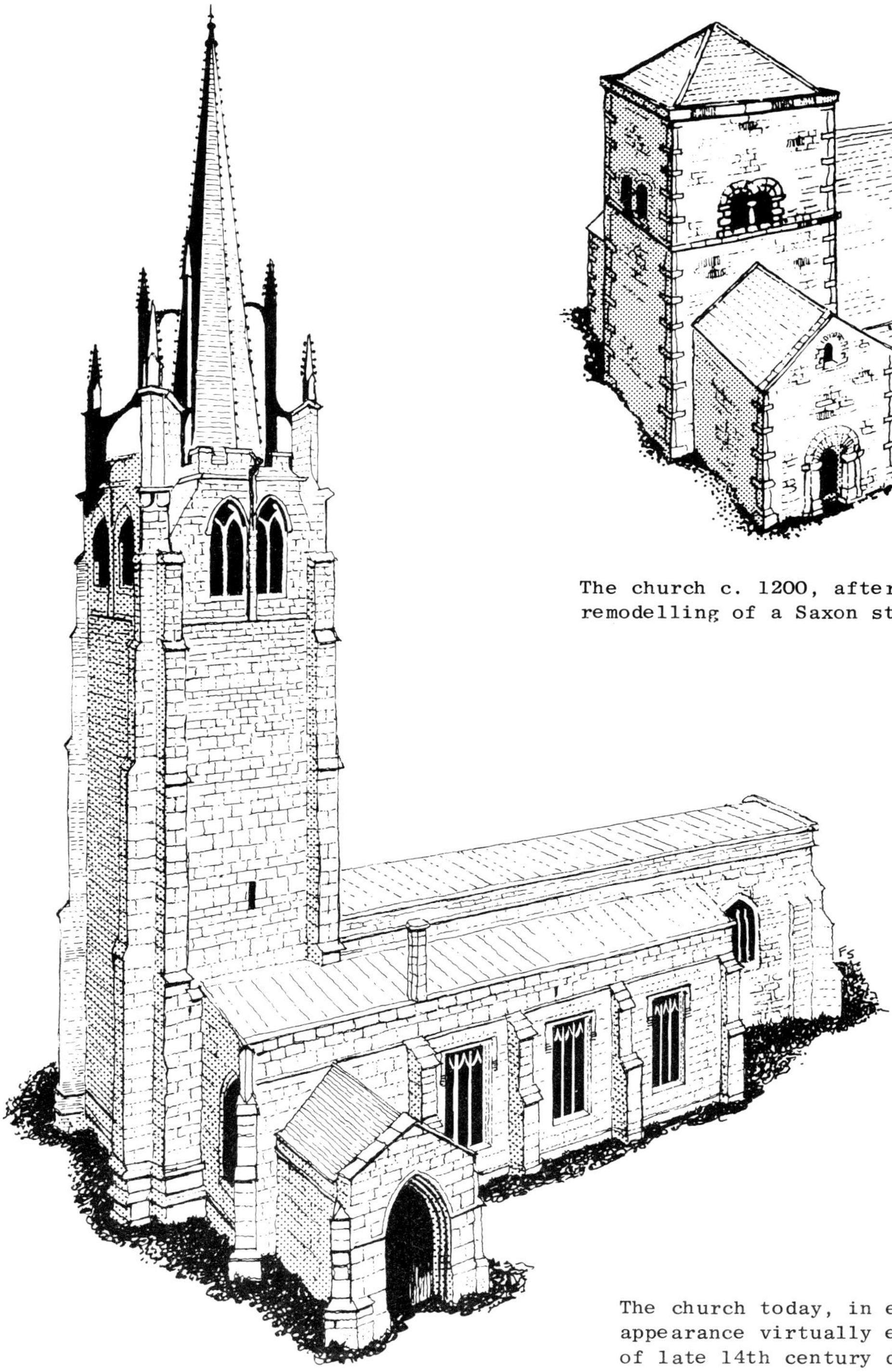

The church today, in external
appearance virtually entirely
of late 14th century date

they in turn are linked by further flying buttresses. The belfry has a pair of openings in each wall, each of two cinquefoiled lights under a pointed head. The upper parts of the newel stair are excessively steep and narrow, although the climb to the parapet is rewarded by an extensive prospect and, more particularly, a fine aerial view of the motte-and-bailey castle adjacent to the churchyard.

POST-MEDIEVAL ALTERATIONS

Laughton church has suffered less alteration and restoration than most of the old parish churches in South Yorkshire, remaining very much in its late 14th century form. The only addition has been the vestry on the north side of the chancel. The doorway into this from the chancel has a slightly segmental arched head of one continuous chamfered order, and a depressed rear arch, suggesting a late 17th century or even an 18th century date. To this date also the windows, a two-light opening on the east and a single rectangular light on the north, can be ascribed.

In the mid 19th century the church was restored by Sir Giles Gilbert Scott who replaced the old nave roof and removed a wooden gallery from under the tower. In 1895 the north aisle wall, which was being undermined by a spring and leaning dangerously, was taken down, underpinned, and rebuilt, each stone being numbered. Presumably this rebuilding did not extend to the west end of the wall with its Saxon door. This work has left no visual evidence, the wall now appearing wholly of medieval date, with the possible exception of the east window of the aisle, above the vestry roof, which is of rather unusual form, three lights divided by a stepped transom, beneath a triangular rather than an arched head. This may be earlier 19th century work.

NON-STRUCTURAL FEATURES OF INTEREST

THE FONT

The Font beneath the tower is a fine late medieval specimen probably coeval with the remodelling of the church, and has an octagonal embattled bowl with panels of tracery motifs including cusped trefoils and whirling mouchettes.

On the floor beside the font is a small sandstone bowl cut in a block 1 ft. 1 in. (0.33 m.) square, with a vertical roll moulding on each angle and crude carving on each face. Three faces appear to show a pair of arches, the fourth a motif difficult to interpret. The crudity and simplicity of this carving suggest a Saxo-Norman Overlap date.

SCREENS

The lower part of a stone rood screen of Perpendicular date remains *in situ* at the entrance to the chancel. It has an embattled top and recessed rectangular panels. A similar section of screen, now set along the south side of the chancel, almost certainly divided the chancel from the chantry chapel in the east bay of the north aisle.

MEDIEVAL SEPULCHRAL MONUMENTS

Several medieval cross slabs are preserved in Laughton church:

(i) A complete cross slab floor stone in good condition, now standing behind the font. "Masonry" base and a floriated cross of identical design to one on an inscribed slab, dated 1480, at Beighton. The border panel of the Laughton slab is, unusually, blank. Possibly an inscription may have been painted on.

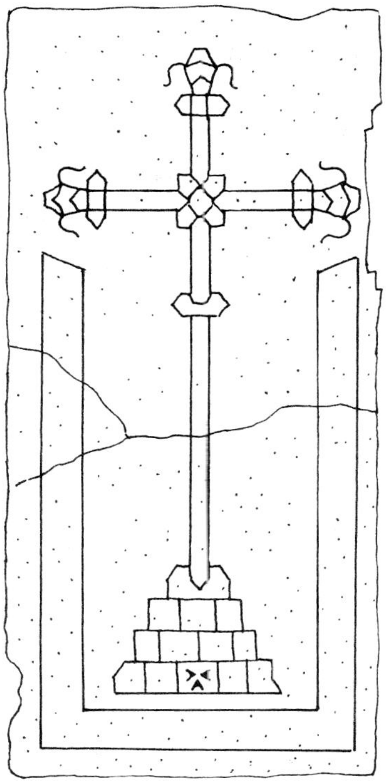

(i)

(ii) Cross slab floor stone in the floor of the south aisle, alongside the south wall midway along the aisle. Very worn. Traces of floriated cross and a few words of marginal inscription, ("hic iace ... quonda ...").

(iii) Fragment of cross slab floor stone in floor at the north-west corner of the tower. "Masonry" base.

(iv) Fragment of cross slab floor stone in floor at the east end of the south aisle. "Masonry" base.

(v) Cross slab re-used as the inner lintel of the north door,(that is the medieval door inserted in the larger Saxon opening). Cross with 'round-leaf' terminals, and on left of shaft an unusually broad-bladed pair of shears. Date probably c. 1250 - 1300.

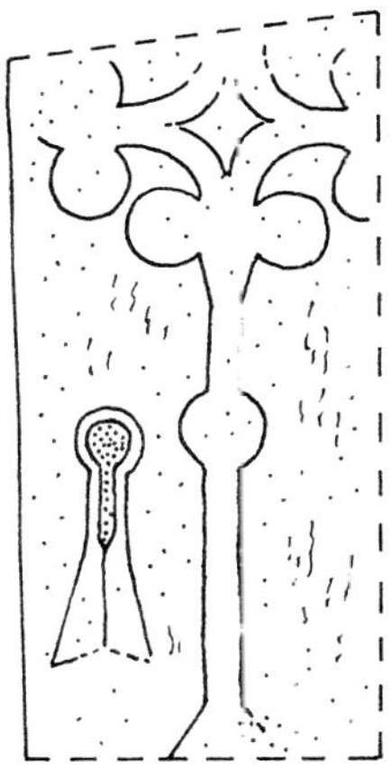

(v)

(vi) Slab on floor of south aisle, against the south wall just east of the eastern window in the wall. Black letter rim inscription, in English. Morris[13] reads: "... she was fyrst maryed to George ... Esquyer and wyth hym she had to chyldran and after ...". The stone has decayed further and the first few words recorded by Morris are no longer legible. The "to" of "to chyldran" looks more like the roman numeral "iv" or even "xv".

(vii) Slab on the floor of the north aisle between the eastern two windows in the aisle wall (not counting that now lighting the organ chamber). A much worn slab with a rim inscription and perhaps some form of design. Morris[14] reads: "Hic iacet corpus Johannis ... oblet qui obiit ix die me(n)si ...".

There are a considerable number of interesting 17th and early 18th century stones incorporated in the paving of the church, many of them rapidly decaying.

ALTAR SLAB

The wooden altar at the east end of the south aisle stands on a medieval altar slab found beneath the floor nearby. The five incised crosses are still visible.

THE BELLS

One of the four bells in the tower is of medieval date, bearing the inscription "AVE MARIA GRATIA PLENA DOMINUS TECUM". Two others bear the inscriptions "Will Boler 1704" and "Jesu be our spede 1621".

CARVED STONES

(A) Built into the internal face of the north wall of the north aisle, 6 ft. 7 ins. (2.00 m.) above floor level and just to the west of the second window from the west, is a stone which might be either part of a free-standing cross, or a grave cover, of 13th century date. The chamfer on either side has large dog-tooth ornament, whilst a line of smaller nail-head runs down the centre.

(B) Built into the external face of the east wall of the chancel, a stone with a simple geometrical pattern of large triangles, incised. Possibly of early Norman or Overlap date.

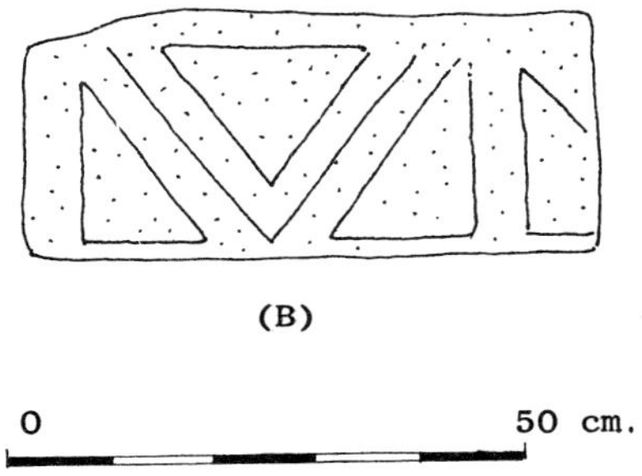

(B)

REFERENCES

1. Taylor, H. M. and Taylor, J. — *Anglo-Saxon Architecture*, I, 375. Cambridge University Press. 1965

2. Lynam, C. — Laughton-en-le-Morthen Church, Yorkshire, *Journal of the British Archaeological Association*, 2nd series 10 (1904), 196

3. Rigby, T. — Ibid., 189

4. Taylor, H. M. and Taylor, J. — Op. cit., 375

5. Taylor, H. M. and Taylor, J. — Op. cit., 375

6. Rigby, T. — Op. cit., 190

7. Rigby, T. — Op. cit., 192

8. Pevsner, N. — *The Buildings of England: Yorkshire, the West Riding*. 300. 2nd edn. Harmondsworth: Penguin 1967

9. Pevsner, N. — Ibid. 300

10. Pevsner, N. — Ibid. 301

11. Hunter, J. — *South Yorkshire*, I, plate facing p.286. London: Nicholls, 1831

12. Pevsner, N. — Op. cit., 300

13. Morris, J. — *The West Riding of Yorkshire* (Little Guide Series) 333. 2nd edn. London: Methuen & Co. 1923

St. Bartholomew's Church, Maltby

Maltby parish church lies low, in a wooded valley cutting through the Magnesian Limestone escarpment, beside a large spring. The old village to the north of the church expanded in size greatly in the 19th and 20th centuries with the development of local collieries.
Only the west tower of the church is ancient, the remainder having been totally rebuilt in 1859. Antiquaries had already realised that the tower was of early date, and it was presumably this that prompted its survival.

DESCRIPTION OF THE TOWER

The west tower measures c. 12 ft. 2 ins. (3.7 m.) by 11 ft. 2 ins. (3.4 m.) internally, with walls 3 ft. 0 in. (0.95 m.) in thickness, constructed of Magnesian Limestone rubble, with occasional courses set diagonally in herringbone fashion. Two string courses of square section form slight set backs, dividing the tower externally into three stages. The original masonry survives to midway up the third stage, a height of c. 47 ft. 7 ins. (14.5 m.) above ground level. The walls above this, with parapet and spire, appear to be 15th century work.
The western angle quoins of the tower are of side-alternate type but of no great size; average height 1 ft. 0 in. (0.3 m.), and of sandstone. The original quoins survive only to a height of a little over 9 ft. 10 ins. (3.0 m.), having been replaced above this by limestone blocks, probably of 19th century date.
The present lofty tower arch and the four-light west window, are plainly Victorian. Several original openings do, however, survive. The lower stage has a blocked round-headed window on the south with its external sill 7 ft. 10 ins. (2.4 m.) above ground level 3 ft. 8 ins. (0.44 m.) wide externally splaying to 3 ft. 8 ins. (1.12 m.) on the internal face of the wall. The rear arch appears to have seen some modification, its east jamb appearing to be set inside the line of the arched head. Higher in the walls of this stage are narrower windows of similar form on both north and south, originally lighting a first floor as the sockets for two floor beams can be recognised internally both on north and south. The voussoirs around the outer openings of these windows are of rubble. The lower window on the south does not really have voussoirs in the strict sense of the word, simply appearing as an opening cut through a rubble wall. On the west, any original windows have been destroyed by the insertion of the large Victorian window.
The second stage of the tower has round-headed single light windows to south, west and north, rather taller than those below and with jambs of squared stone and monolithic heads. On the east is a blocked square-headed door, visible from the nave and set centrally above the Victorian tower arch. The jambs of this use several upright stones.
The belfry has a two-light opening in each wall, at first sight looking like rather poor 15th century work, the lights have trefoiled ogee arches under a square head. Closer inspection reveals that these are in fact late medieval remodellings of earlier openings, of which the jambs survive, along with the heavy square block which now forms the base of the mullion

Altar tomb with cross brass, Maltby
This 14th century monument now serves as a coffin rest in the lych gate giving access to the churchyard, and has recently been badly damaged by vandals.
Drawn 25 August 1977

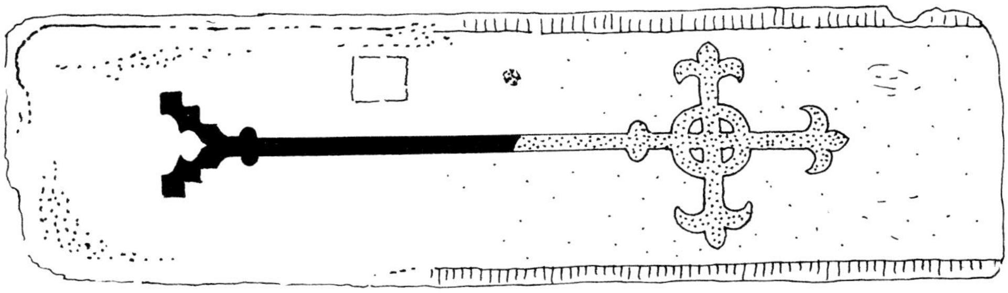

Cross Brass

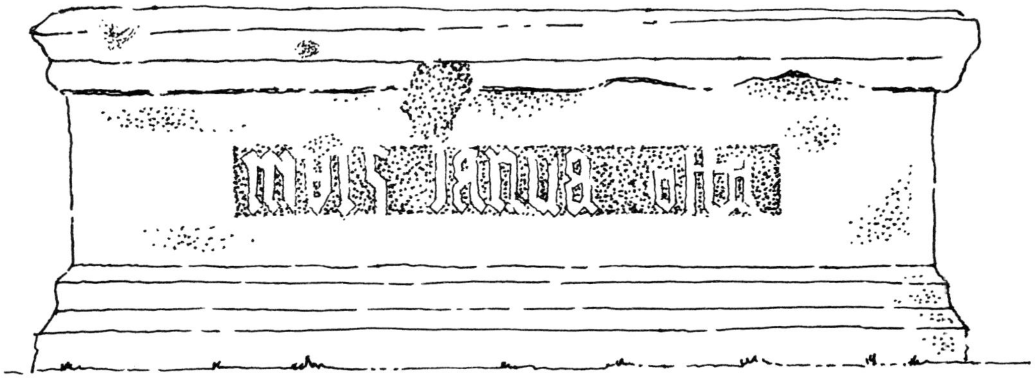

East elevation
(a similar inscribed panel on the west has been erased by weathering)

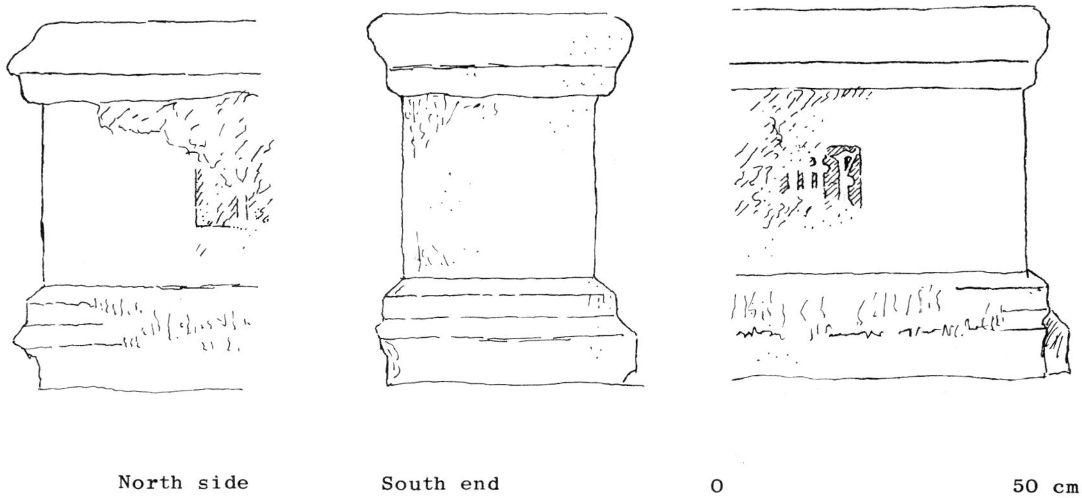

North side

South end
(North end similar)

0 50 cm.

dividing the lights. This is almost certainly the base of a former mid-wall shaft. Above the belfry openings a distinct change in masonry type marks the 15th century rebuilding of the top of the tower. The simple crenellated parapet and short octagonal stone spire are of this date.

THE DATE OF THE TOWER

The tower is difficult to date closely. Morris[1] and Pevsner[2] consider it Early Norman and Norman respectively, but writers of the last century such as Bloxam[3] and Armitage[4] were inclined to recognise pre-Conquest workmanship. Several features do indeed appear to be distinctively Anglo-Saxon in style if not in actual date; the rubble voussoirs and jambs of the windows of the lower stage which are the only example in South Yorkshire of windows of this form, the plain square-section string courses and the original form of the belfry openings.
The second stage windows are less distinctly pre-Conquest in form, although their monolithic heads and the absence of any external splay are Saxon rather than Norman in style. The use of upright stones in the jambs of the high level doorway to the nave, and the position of the doorway, are also suggestive of Saxon building. The interior of the upper stages of the tower has not been inspected, due to its inaccessibility.
The Maltby tower may probably be safely ascribed to the Overlap, tending towards the Saxon rather than the Norman in style. A date somewhere in the 11th century seems likely.

The present belfry openings at Maltby (above), and a reconstruction of their original 11th century form (below).

THE BODY OF THE CHURCH

No detailed description of the body of the church pulled down in 1859 has as yet been traced, and no feature from it seems to have been incorporated in its Victorian successor, Hunter, writing thirty years before the rebuilding[5] describes the church as a "small and rather mean building" of nave, chancel and south aisle, with the west tower. The medieval roof appears to have survived, as he gives the names of "some early benefactors" painted on its rafters:

Thomas Forrester,
Agnes Forrester,
Dominus Clifford,
... Townend de Maltby, clericus.
John Townend, of Maltby, gyver of thys tymbar.

NON-STRUCTURAL FEATURES

(i) The Font stands at the west end of the nave. The plain octagonal bowl looks like late medieval work, of 14th or 15th century date. The shaft and base appear to be more recent.

(ii) One interesting medieval sepluchral monument survives in the form of an altar tomb bearing a cross slab inlaid in brass. This now forms the coffin rest in the centre of the lych gate giving access to the churchyard and is suffering badly from modern vandalism. The brass of the cross design has been almost entirely torn off. A monument such as this, unique in South Yorkshire, should really be kept inside the church. The cross is of 14th century form with an ogee arch beneath the stepped Calvary base. The tomb beneath has had an inscribed panel on each long face. That now facing east reads:

mors janua vitae

(death, the gateway to life)

The west-facing panel has weathered into illegibility.

(iii) The only other medieval fragment is part of a door jamb re-used as a coping stone on the wall on the west side of the churchyard. This has a quarter-round moulding suggesting a 14th century date.

REFERENCES

1. Morris, J. E. *The West Riding of Yorkshire* (Little Guide Series) 349. 2nd edn. London: Methuen & Co. 1923

2. Pevsner, N. *The Buildings of England: Yorkshire, the West Riding,* 359. 2nd edn. Harmondsworth: Penguin 1967

3. Bloxam, M. H. *The Principles of Gothic Ecclesiastical Architecture,* 76, 11th edn. London: George Bell & Sons 1882

4. Armitage, E. S. *A Key to English Antiquities,* 259. Sheffield: William Townsend, 1897

5. Hunter, J. *South Yorkshire,* I, 264. Nicholls & Son, 1831

A Gazetteer of Medieval Parish Churches in South Yorkshire

In the brief notes on each church, especial reference is made to any surviving fabric or sculpture of pre-Conquest, Overlap or early Norman date.

ADWICK-LE-STREET, ST. LAWRENCE SE541086
Norman nave and chancel with later medieval north aisle, chapel and west tower, all over-restored in 1862. Most of the windows are Victorian. Much restored Norman south door and remains of a window of the same date in the chancel.

ADWICK-UPON-DEARNE, ST. JOHN SE470015
Pebbledash externally and plaster within make this small church disappointing to the archaeologist. A plain Norman chancel arch has been replaced this century by a modern 'Gothic' version. The bell-cote is said to be Norman, and the south door is probably 12th century.

ARKSEY, ALL SAINTS SE 579069
A large cruciform church with an impressive 13th century crossing tower and quite a number of structural puzzles. The transepts are early Norman, and two distinct builds are discernible in them. Thinly coursed stone is used in the lower courses of the south transept and internal faces of the lower parts of the north, with much squarer stone above. The east end, despite Pevsner's claim, is garish Victorian pseudo-Norman work.

ARMTHORPE, ST. MARY AND ST. LEONARD SE622049
Norman nave and chancel, but the north aisle and most of the windows date from 1885. The very plain chancel arch may be early Norman, the nave south door is work of c.1200. Two original Norman windows survive on the south of the nave.

ASTON, ALL SAINTS SK468853
The nave arcades are late Norman/Transitional, with round-headed arches. Decorated and Perpendicular windows, much 19th century restoration.

AUSTERFIELD, ST. HELENA SK662947
An attractive small Norman church, with a good chancel arch and south door, the latter having an interesting tympanum carved with a dragon. Transitional north arcade, the aisle walls themselves a 19th century rebuild.

BARNBURGH, ST. PETER SE484032
The earliest part of the church is the Norman west tower, heightened in the 15th century. Much Decorated and Perpendicular work. Inside the church a piece of a sculptured cross shaft of overlap date and the memorable canopied tomb of Percival Cresacre (1477) with a variety of

decoration and inscriptions. The oak effigy resting beneath the canopy is an early 14th century piece.

BARNBY DUN, ST. PETER AND ST. PAUL SE614097
Nave and aisles good early 14th century work, Perpendicular tower and Victorian chancel. At the south-east angle of the nave is an unusual feature, a stair turret housing the narrowest of newel stairs, giving access not only to the rood loft but also to the roof.

BARNSLEY, ST. MARY SE343067
Rebuilt in 1820-1821, except for a Perpendicular west tower.

BAWTRY, ST. NICHOLAS SK653930
The architectural history of this church has never been properly explained, the north aisle wall especially is a puzzle. The blocked north door is late Norman. West tower post-medieval Gothic of 1712-1713.

BEIGHTON, ST. MARY SK443833
Mostly Perpendicular, a church which suffered heavily at the hands of the Victorian restorers. The Norman chancel arch is their work, although said to be a copy of an original of which only fragments remained.

BOLTON-UPON-DEARNE, ST. ANDREW SE456025
See text.

BRADFIELD, ST. NICHOLAS SK267925
A good 'Pennine Perpendicular' church with a huge moorland parish. A little earlier medieval work is incorporated. In the north aisle stands a very plain stone cross, probably pre-Conquest, which does not originate from the church but was found near the Cross Inn at Low Bradfield.

BRAITHWELL, ST. JAMES SK530947
The south doorway is a simple early Norman piece with an interesting tympanum carved with a variety of geometrical motifs. The remainder of the church is mostly 13th and 14th century work: crossing arches suggest that it was intended to erect a central tower, but the present tower, Perpendicular, is at the west end.

BRODSWORTH, ST. MICHAEL SE507072
See text, chapter 4.

BURGHWALLIS, ST. HELEN SE537120
See text, chapter 4.

CAMPSALL, ST. MARY MAGDALENE SE545141
A large and interesting church. Evidence of an aisleless nave, probably pre-Conquest in date, can be seen on the internal face of the south wall of the nave where remains of the eastern quoins and some adjacent herringbone work (both reminiscent of Burghwallis) are exposed.

The nave was extended eastwards and given transepts in the first of two phases of Norman reconstruction, the nave, aisles and spectacular west tower dating from the second. Much later medieval work, good rood screen and various 12th century and later sculptured pieces and sepulchral monuments.

CANTLEY, ST. WILFRID SE619014
The situation of the church is interesting, away from the village, set on a mound, and orientated a long way north of east. The building is heavily Victorianised, but retains some medieval features, the earliest being the priest's door on the south side of the chancel which looks Norman, with a segmental head set under a semicircular arch.

CAWTHORNE, ALL SAINTS
Perhaps the main interest here is the pre-Conquest sculpture, two sections of a cross in the reconstructed cross in the churchyard west of the church, and a second cross head built into the external face of the east gable of the north chapel. Inside the church an Overlap font bowl with good carving. The building itself is mostly 19th century, but old work survives notably in the north chapel and the Perpendicular west tower.

CONISBROUGH, ST. PETER SK512988
See text, chapter 4.

DARFIELD, ALL SAINTS SE419043
Another church of which the architectural history needs thoroughly investigating. The earliest section is the west tower, the lower section Overlap or early Norman, of rubble with mixed side-alternate and face-alternate quoins, and quite massive, being 21 ft. 4 ins. (6.5 m.) square internally. The tower arch is a puzzle, the jambs semicircular shafts of 12th century style carrying a pointed arch which cuts through the lower part of a high-level doorway; this has a shouldered arched head. Two round-headed windows have similar shouldered rear arches. The upper part of the tower is late medieval, perhaps replacing an earlier timber belfry (c.f. Brodsworth and Hooton Pagnell). Re-used in the church walls are two pieces of pre-Conquest sculpture, in the internal face of the south wall of the tower c. 16 ft. 5 ins. (5 m.) off the floor, and in the vestry north of the chancel, in the internal face of the south wall just above floor level. Built into the internal face of the south wall of the nave above the western respond of the arcade is what appears to be the monolithic head of an early window, set upside down.

DARTON, ALL SAINTS SE311099
Another Perpendicular church on the Pennine fringe. The chancel is dated by an inscription on the wall-plate stating that it was completed in 1517 by Thomas Tickhill, Prior of Monk Bretton.

DONCASTER, ST. GEORGE SE574036
An impressive Victorian church on the site of a fine medieval building destroyed by fire in 1853. The only relic that survives of this latter is a vaulted crypt, roofed with medieval cross slabs, beneath the modern vestry and organ chamber.

ECCLESFIELD, ST. MARY SK353942

Once called 'The Minster of the Moors', another 'Pennine Perpendicular' edifice typical of the western part of the county. A little earlier work is incorporated. In the south transept is a late Saxon or Overlap cross shaft found nearby.

EDLINGTON, ST. PETER SK532974

Now redundant as a church, but recently restored, a small building with some quite ornate Norman work. The south door is unusual, with zigzag and beak-head ornament carried down the jambs to the ground without any impost. Norman chancel arch and nave window.

FINNINGLEY, ST. OSWALD SK670992

An interesting church with quite spectacular medieval roofs to nave and chancel. The west tower is early Norman, with a very plain tower arch and double belfry openings. The main problem is the south door, which must be early but is quite different in style to the tower; a semicircular arched head with a heavy roll moulding, carried on block capitals with some crude carving in apparent pre-Conquest style. Even more distinctively Saxon is the stripwork which continues the line of the hoodmould beyond the imposts to floor level. Is the doorway the product of a mason schooled in Saxon styles working perhaps at the end of the 11th century, whilst his Norman counterparts produced the tower? Or is it a relic of an earlier church?

FISHLAKE, ST. CUTHBERT SE656132

A spacious and impressive church, mostly late medieval, but with a splendidly ornate late Norman south door which Pevsner calls 'perhaps the most lavishly decorated in Yorkshire'. There is also some fine Decorated and Perpendicular work.

FRICKLEY, ALL SAINTS SE468079

Now standing alone amidst the fields, the church of a deserted medieval village. Externally the building looks almost all Victorian, but inside is a good Norman chancel arch, its shafted responds set high as if to come above a screen.

HANDSWORTH, ST. MARY SK411862

A church that has seen much 19th century alteration. The chancel is largely 13th century, with lancet windows and good sedilia. The abnormal height of the north arcade is due to later modifications allowing the insertion of a gallery.

HARTHILL, ALL HALLOWS SK494810

The arcades are of c. 1200, the north with round arches, the south with pointed. Externally, it is apparent at the west end that the aisles have been added to an earlier nave of which the quoins are visible, but not of a distinctive enough form to date. Some later medieval work. The Victorians inserted the pseudo-Norman windows in the north aisle which Pevsner rightly describes as 'horrible'.

HATFIELD, ST. LAWRENCE SE663096

A large cruciform church with a good central tower, mostly Perpendicular. Earlier rubble masonry apparent in the west front and aisle walls which preserve Norman west and south doors.

Finningley
The South Door.

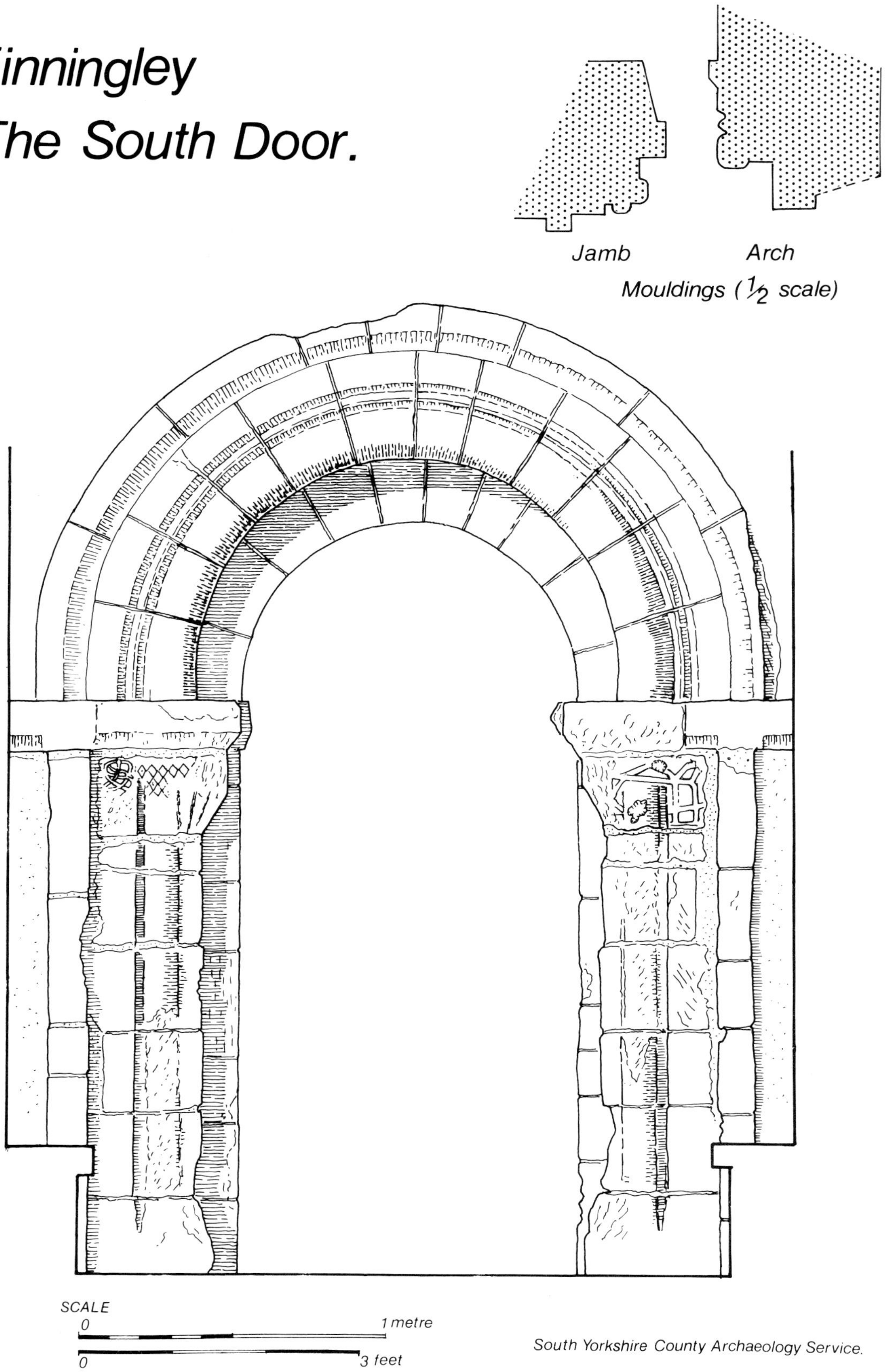

South Yorkshire County Archaeology Service.

HICKLETON, ST. WILFRID SE483053

Externally a completely Perpendicular building, pinnacled and embattled. Inside, half hidden by a forest of struts and supports counteracting mining subsidence, a Norman chancel arch with zigzag.

HIGH HOYLAND, ALL HALLOWS SE275107

Now redundant, set in a near-circular hilltop churchyard away from the village. Only a 13th or 14th century arch on the north side of the nave remains from the medieval building. The west tower is interesting post-medieval Gothic of 1679, the rest early 20th century. Built into the north wall of the nave internally are a series of sculptured stones including some pre-Conquest pieces. A good cross head was stolen from here recently, evidence of an unhappy modern trend. The font from this church is now at Skelmanthorpe, across the border into West Yorkshire, and is an interesting Overlap piece similar to that at Cawthorne.

HIGH MELTON, ST. JAMES SE509018

An attractive little hilltop church. The nave, unusually tall with relatively thin 2 ft. 6 ins. (0.75 m.) walls, is probably of pre-Conquest date, and measures 23 ft. 4 ins. (7.1 m.) by c. 14 ft. 9 ins. (4.5 m.) internally. The only angle quoin visible, at the north-west corner, is irregular but includes some unusually tall stones. No original architectural features survive. The south arcade and chancel arch are Norman, the rest of the church later medieval. There is a good collection of cross slabs and sculptural fragments, one or two of which may be quite early but nothing distinctively Saxon.

High Melton,
The nave from the north-west.

HOOTON PAGNELL, ALL SAINTS SE485079

See text, chapter 4.

HOOTON ROBERTS, ST. JOHN THE BAPTIST SK484971

A small church with some Norman or Transitional work, much Victorianised. A small cross slab at the west end of the nave may be of late 11th century date.

KIRK BRAMWITH, ST. MARY SE620117

A church consisting of nave, chancel and west tower. The Norman south door and chancel arch both have scalloped capitals and zigzag. Some later medieval features, tower heightened in the 15th century.

KIRK SANDALL, ST. OSWALD SE609081

No longer in use. The nave and chancel, internal dimensions 28 ft. 11 ins. (8.8 m.) by 16 ft. 9 ins. (5.1 m.) and 17 ft. 3 ins. (5.25 m.) by 11 ft. 10 ins. (3.6 m.) respectively, represent a small Overlap church, with walls of a mixture of Magnesian Limestone rubble and brownish river cobbles, only 2 ft. 7 ins. (0.78 m.) thick, and rough side alternate quoins of no great size. In the west gable are two or three herringbone courses. No architectural features survive from this first phase, but the added south aisle, retaining two windows and its south door, is a late 12th century addition. Its very similar fabric and quoins suggest

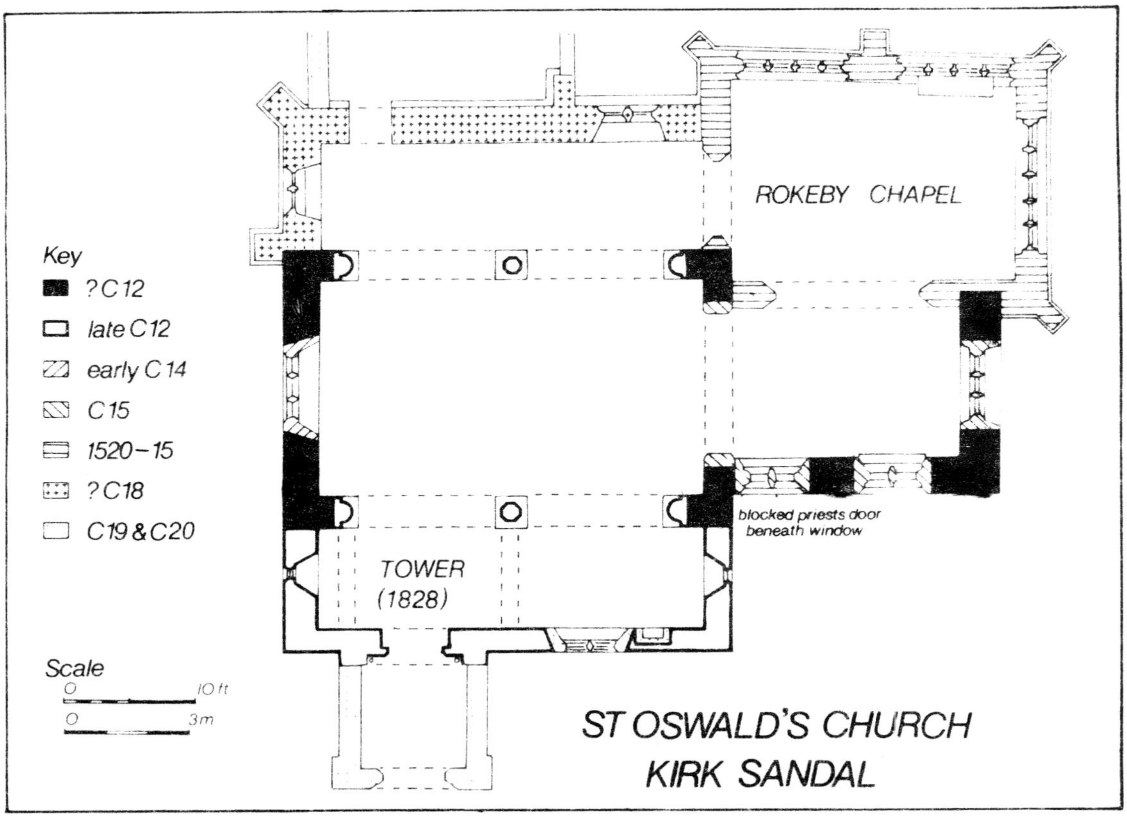

that the nave and chancel may not be much earlier in date. Of the later medieval work, the Rokeby Chapel on the north of the chancel, dated by documentary evidence to 1510-1520, is impressive late Perpendicular. The peculiar tower over the south aisle is an addition of 1828, lowered in 1935.

LAUGHTON-EN-LE-MORTHEN, ALL SAINTS SK517882

See text, chapter 4.

LETWELL, ST. PETER SK559871

Burnt down in 1867 and rebuilt in 1869, the only medieval fabric to survive is in the Perpendicular west tower and the external face of the north wall of the nave, the two western bays of which are of ashlar with a blocked round-headed door (badly damaged and of uncertain date) and a 15th century window. The eastern bay has a Victorian window, but the walling is of rubble and may be early medieval.

LOVERSALL, ST. KATHARINE SK576987

Much Victorianised, the south aisle and many of the windows are completely 19th century. Some rubble masonry remains visible in the east end of the chancel and inside, in the south wall, the plastered over remains of what looks to be a 12th century window are visible beside the Perpendicular arch to the south chapel. In the churchyard to the south is a very interesting 14th century monument, a cross slab (much weathered) set on a tomb chest, the sides of which are carved with a variety of contemporary tracery patterns as if the mason had had his copy book in front of him.

MALTBY, ST. BARTHOLOMEW SK528919

See text, chapter 4.

MARR, ST. HELEN SE515053

The nave and chancel are early Norman or Overlap, with quite an amount of herringbone masonry, although most of the architectural features are of later medieval date. The west tower has strange arches to north and south now opening into shallow recesses; it was obviously intended to build aisles to engage it.

MEXBOROUGH, ST. JOHN THE BAPTIST SK480997

Some late Norman or Transitional work survives in this much restored church. The three bay north arcade has round unmoulded arches, and some of the chancel lancets are old, the apse being an addition of 1891. Inside is a fragment of a late Saxon cross shaft.

NORTON, ST. JAMES SK359822

The earliest part is the south door, Norman with a shallow segmental arch under a blank tympanum enclosed by a semicircular arch with zigzag, the whole being so much restored that it is difficult to tell how much old work survives. Elsewhere some 13th century work, but the general appearance of the church is largely Perpendicular. Some interesting sepulchral monuments.

OWSTON, ALL SAINTS SE551111

An interesting church with a somewhat complicated building history. The west gable of the nave is Overlap work, evidenced by its herringbone courses. What must be the original west door, altered in its details, now opens into the base of the later Norman tower, and two round-headed windows higher up the wall open into the first floor chamber in the tower. On the west face of the wall they are enclosed under a large round-headed arch carrying a thickening of the wall, a modification contemporary with the addition of the tower. Good Decorated and Perpendicular work elsewhere in the church, and some interesting monuments.

PENISTONE, ST. JOHN THE BAPTIST SE247033

The dimensions of the nave, 63 ft. 10 ins. (19.45 m.) by 19 ft. 8 ins. (6.0 m.) internally, its relatively thin 2 ft. 6 ins. (0.75 m.) walls, and the survival of a few herringbone courses at the east end of the north arcade, suggest that pre-Conquest or Overlap fabric may survive *in situ*. A late Saxon carved stone is built into the north-east angle quoin of the nave. The six bay nave arcades are 13th century work. Many of the windows and the fine west tower are Perpendicular.

RAWMARSH, ST. MARY SK436959

The medieval church here was demolished in 1839 to make way for its Victorian successor. It seems to have been a building of early Norman or Overlap date, as evidenced by an old print and Hunters brief account,'the tower gives the ideas of strength and solidity'. The present building preserves a plain and heavily retooled Norman door, and a 12th century churchyard cross.

ROSSINGTON, ST. MICHAEL SK625984

The body of the church here was rebuilt in 1844 retaining the impressive Norman chancel arch (as at Frickley the shafts start high above floor level implying the existence of a stone screen at some time) and south door, a simple composition of the same date. The tower is Perpendicular.

ROTHERHAM, ALL SAINTS SK429729

One of the most impressive Perpendicular churches in the North of England All Saints dominates the centre of Rotherham with its fine crossing tower and spire. Inside, a diligent search reveals some traces of earlier work. 12th century masonry survives *in situ* in the tower piers, and there are some good Norman capitals re-used in the bases of the arcades (specially constructed trapdoors allow these to be inspected). By lifting a grating on the north side of the north-west tower pier an even more interesting feature is revealed, a section of wall beneath the pier and obviously unrelated to it, containing a door jamb. This is almost certainly pre-Conquest work, but does not reveal much about the church of which it formed part.

ROYSTON, ST. JOHN THE BAPTIST SE364112

Another church virtually entirely Perpendicular in external appearance, some Decorated work within but apparently nothing earlier. The oriel window on the west side of the tower is an unusual, and striking, feature.

SHEFFIELD, CATHEDRAL OF ST. PETER AND ST. PAUL SK354875

The parish church until 1914, and now hardly the most impressive of England's cathedrals. The central tower with its crocketted spire and parts of the chancel are medieval, the usual Perpendicular of the area. Some re-used 12th century architectural fragments in the north chapel. The nave is Victorian and the west end more recent.

SILKSTONE, ALL SAINTS SE291058

A 'Pennine Perpendicular' church externally, a thorough remodelling of an earlier cruciform building. References survive to the taking down of the old central tower in 1479 and the completion of the present west tower in 1495. The responds of the chancel arch and the arch into the present north chapel survive from the old crossing, and are of later 12th century date.

SKELBROOKE, ST. MICHAEL SE511121

Virtually everything is Victorian, after an 1872 rebuilding necessitated by a serious fire. The vestiges of the old church which survive suggest that it was an interesting structure. The nave is unusually long and narrow, 44 ft. 4 ins. (13.5 m.) by 16 ft. 7 ins. (5.06 m.) internally, with a west tower which, below the present openings, shows traces of their predecessors which have been of two lights with a central shaft, perhaps of the pre-Conquest form. The walls have all been refaced externally. Inside, a good 14th century canopied niche and a rood loft stair survive in the nave, a 14th century piscina and a two bay 15th century arcade in the chancel.

SOUTH ANSTON, ST. JAMES SK520837

Mostly Decorated and Perpendicular, with an attractive west tower which appears to be a simplified copy on a smaller scale of that at Laughton-en-le-Morthen a few miles away.

SPROTBOROUGH, ST. MARY SE540020

Quite a large church, with many features of interest both in the fabric and monuments etc. The side walls of a short aisleless nave survive above the eastern two bays of the 14th century arcades, the north arcade re-using two late 12th century responds. The remainder of the church is of later Medieval date. Part of a pre-Conquest cross shaft is built into the base of a buttress on the south side of the chancel.

STAINTON, ST. WINIFRED SK555936

The walls of the nave and chancel are probably early Norman, retaining a very simple chancel arch, semicircular, of a single square order, rising from imposts chamfered beneath. Remains of a Norman window and a round-arched priest's door in the south wall of the chancel. Later medieval the south chapel and west tower.

TANKERSLEY, ST. PETER SK350996

Mostly 14th century, although the three bay north arcade may be a century earlier, and the walls of the north aisle were rebuilt in 1881. In the walls of the porch are several interesting 12th century cross slab grave covers and headstones. The rood loft stair is an interesting survival.

THORNE, ST. NICHOLAS SE690133

A church which may have originated (as St. George's at Doncaster seems to have done) as a chapel in the castle bailey. All that remains of the castle now is the Peel Hill across the road to the north of the church, with some foundations on its summit. Remains of several Norman windows can be seen in the chancel. The rest of the church is later medieval of several periods, the 15th century south porch (formerly of two storeys, with an oriel window) and belfry stage of the tower being notable.

THORPE SALVIN, ST. PETER SK520812

Norman and later. Of the 12th century work the south door and chancel arch are good examples. An attractive church which has not suffered too heavily from 'restorations'. The Norman font is the most interesting feature. One of the finest in the country, it bears representations of a baptism and of the four seasons under round-headed arches.

THROAPHAM, ST. JOHN SK523876

An interesting church, now rarely used and in poor repair, at the opposite end of the long village street of Laughton-en-le-Morthen to the parish church of All Saints. The north, south and east walls of the nave, only 2 ft. 2 ins. (0.65 m.) wide, survive from an aisleless church of pre-Conquest or Overlap date, enlarged by the addition of aisles and the rebuilding of the chancel c. 1200. The arcades now terminate in half arches at their west ends, suggesting that the original nave was truncated when the present Perpendicular west tower was built. In 1709 the chancel was completely rebuilt and the south porch added, and the building was further interfered with by the Victorians. Some interesting sepulchral monuments, notably an ornate

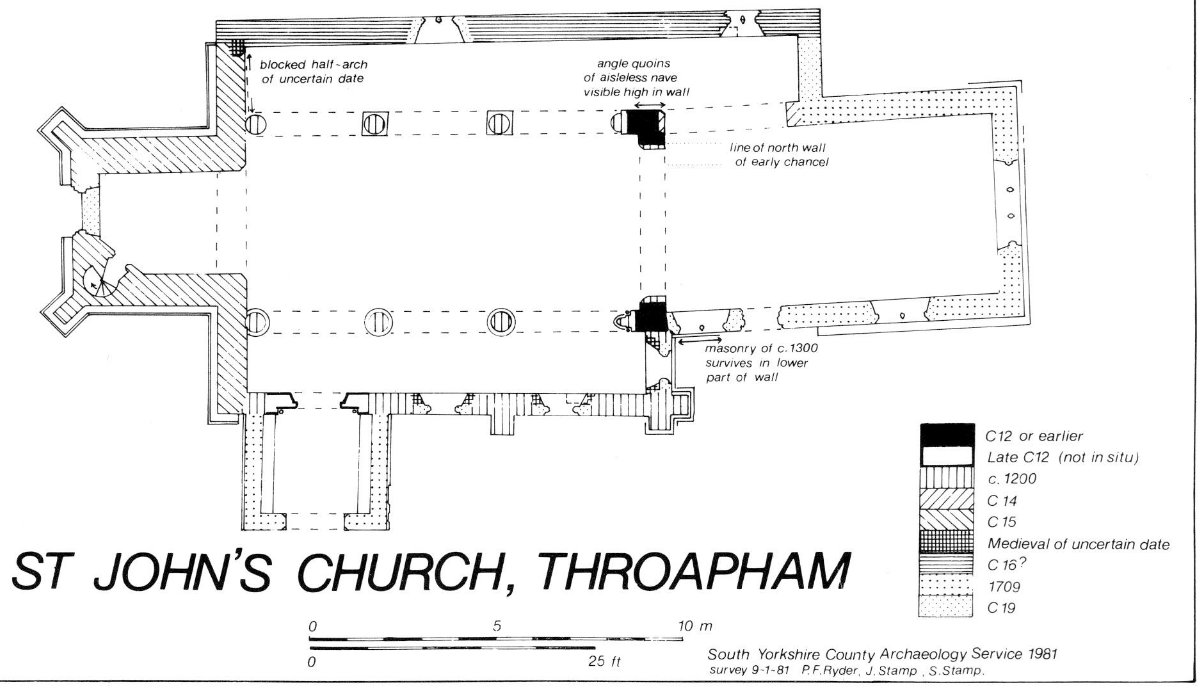

ST JOHN'S CHURCH, THROAPHAM

cross slab carved in high relief, and a good cross slab floor stone of the early 15th century with, unusually, its inscription in English rather than Latin.

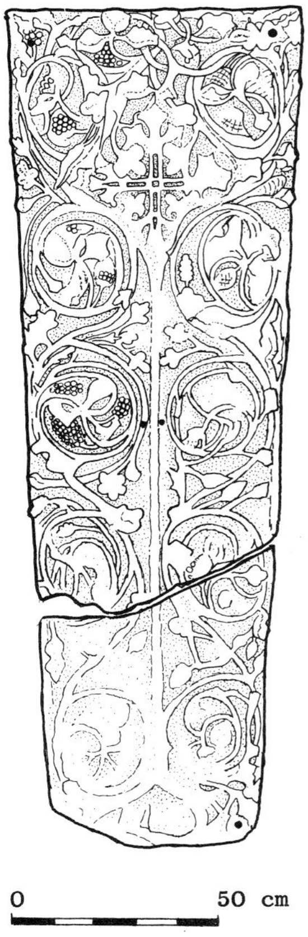

Throapham, Cross Slab

THRYBERGH, ST. LEONARD SK467955

Another church which has suffered many vicissitudes and 'restorations' but which preserves some early fabric. The walls of the nave, and perhaps part of the north wall of the chancel, are probably of Overlap date, built of rubble with rough side-alternate quoins of no great size. At the west end of the north wall of the chancel are traces of herringbone work. The only feature to survive is the lower part of a doorway, beneath the western of the two large windows in the south wall. This early nave was lengthened westwards in the 12th century, the extension being built in ashlar. Its blocked north door survives. St. Leonard's Cross, now in the churchyard south-east of the church, but brought there only relatively recently from a site at the east end of the village, is a good specimen of Overlap sculpture, with both pre- and post-Conquest motifs.

THURNSCOE, ST. HELEN SE450057

The west tower of 1729 has on the west side of its lowest stage a medieval church. The rest of the building is Victorian. Some fragments of medieval sculpture inside, at the east end of the south aisle.

TICKHILL, ST. MARY SK592931

A 13th century and later building, thought to have replaced the pre-Conquest church of Dadsley, a mile or so to the north, when the present settlement grew up around the Norman castle. Good

Early English work in the lower part of the impressive west tower and the chancel. The rest is Perpendicular, dating from a major remodelling of the church commenced c. 1350. Some interesting medieval monuments inside.

TODWICK, ST. PETER AND ST. PAUL SK498841

A small but interesting church with a pre-Conquest or Overlap aisleless nave, later medieval west tower and south porch, and a post-medieval chancel. The nave has walls of coursed red sandstone (the same material the Saxon builders used at nearby Laughton). All the angle quoins have been rebuilt with the exception of the lower part of the south eastern, which shows good side-alternate work. The blocked north door, although partly reconstructed at some later date, shows some features which are stylistically pre-Conquest. The semicircular chancel arch might either be Overlap or Norman, but has been subject to much alteration.

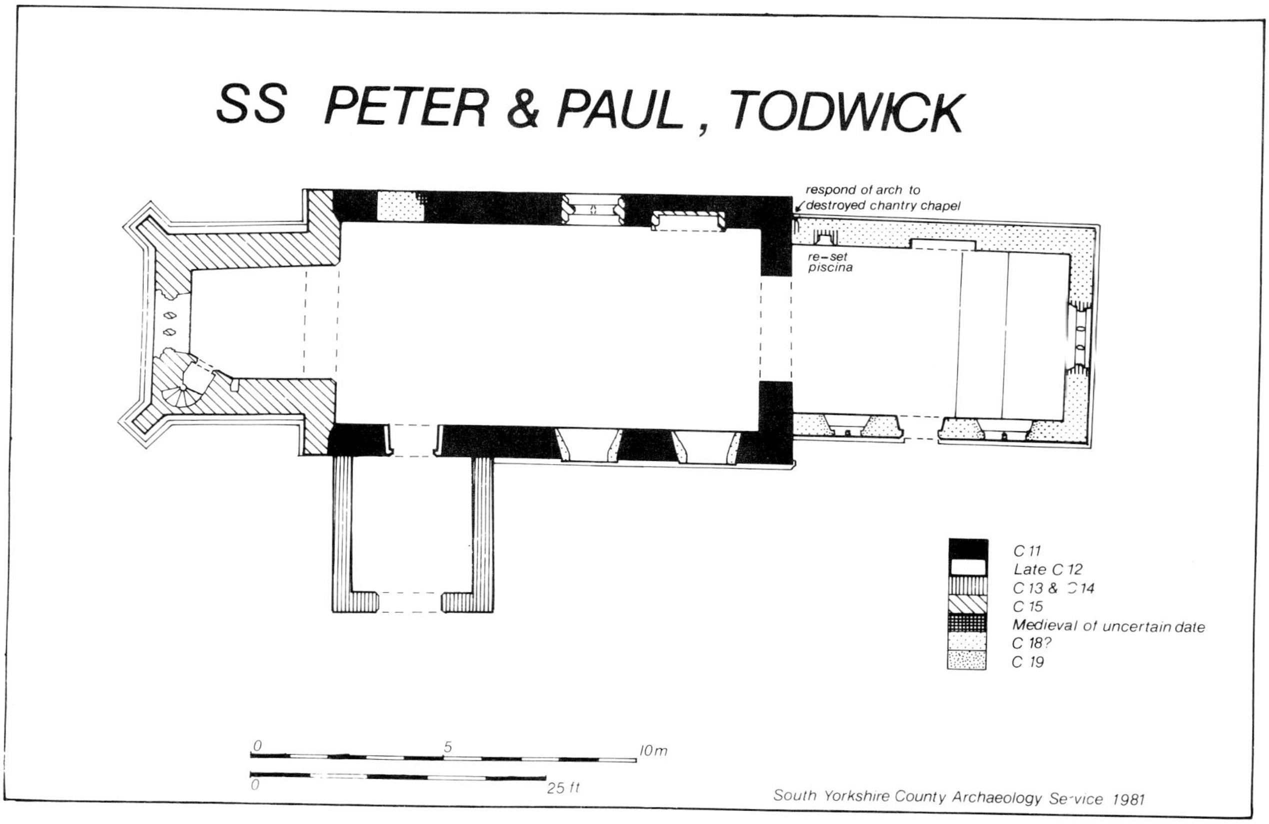

TREETON, ST. HELEN SK432877

A church which Pevsner terms "a confusing building", Early English and later, tower with a Perpendicular top strangely placed at the west end of the south aisle. Some interesting monuments, including a very fine cross slab set upright behind the pulpit.

WADWORTH, ST. JOHN THE BAPTIST SK569971

Quite a large and impressive church. The earliest work is the late Norman arcading on the internal walls of the south porch and south aisle, showing that by the end of the 12th century the church had almost attained its present dimensions. Some good Decorated and Perpendicular work, and interesting sepulchral monuments.

WALES, ST. JOHN THE BAPTIST SK478827

A two-cell Norman church, quite early, with the usual Perpendicular west tower, reduced in status in 1897 to the north aisle of a large Victorian building. The surviving north and east walls of the original building are of rubble, with irregular but quite large angle quoins, and some very large stones used in the lower courses of the north nave wall. The Norman chancel arch, with zigzag, and south door (re-set in 1897 on the south side of the new building) survive, the latter having a segmental lintel with a tympanum above decorated with a chequer pattern, enclosed by a band of lozenges and a semicircular arch with crude beakhead ornament. All in all one of the most impressive early 12th century doors in the county.

WARMSWORTH, ST. PETER SE551012

The last church to stand on this site was an early 19th century structure pulled down in the early 1940's. In the winter of 1977 to 1978 excavation revealed the footings of a small two-cell Norman church and some sculptured stones (now in Doncaster Museum) including part of a Norman grave cover with similar incised geometrical patterns to those on the tympanum at Braithwell.

WATH-UPON-DEARNE, ALL SAINTS SE433009

An interesting church with several architectural problems. The north wall of the nave and west part of the north wall of the chancel are part of a late Saxon or Overlap church, both pierced by Norman arcades. Three large side-alternate quoins at the base of the north-east angle of the nave survive. On the north side of the north wall of the chancel, to the east of the two bay arcade to the Lady Chapel, the ends of the stones of the north-east chancel quoin can be seen (proving that the original chancel was not apsidal). On the south side of the north wall of the nave, above the obviously 19th century opening to the east of the arcade, is a blocked square-headed door (to the rood loft?) with some upright stones in its jambs, suggesting that it may be of quite early date. The western quoins of the nave are of smaller stones than the north-eastern, and may be a later rebuild, perhaps coeval with the tower (early 12th century?). This has belfry openings (now blocked up) of early form having twin round-headed lights without an enclosing arch, divided by a mid-wall shaft. The belfry stage is a Perpendicular addition.

A small stone now on the sill of the west window of the Lady Chapel has some crude carving on it, difficult to make sense of, which may be pre-Conquest work.

WENTWORTH, HOLY TRINITY SK384983

The old church now consists of a Perpendicular west tower, the ruins of the south wall of the nave (Renaissance work of 1684) and the restored chancel and north chapel, which incorporate some medieval work. There are also some interesting sepulchral monuments. Built into the internal face of the east wall of the north chapel is a stone with an arcade of intersecting arches and a series of triangular panels. The stone is probably part of an early 12th century grave cover, perhaps of coped form. The 12th century capitals in the chapel are known to have been imported from Monk Bretton Priory after the Dissolution, to be used in the nave arcade which was pulled down at the end of the 19th century.

WHISTON, ST. MARY MAGDALENE SK451900

In 1883 the old church was converted into the south aisle of a new building. The old nave is 12th century work, with a west window now covered by the slightly later west tower.

WICKERSLEY, ST. ALBAN SK478917

The body of the church is a 19th century rebuild, the only medieval work being the lower three stages of the west tower, late 15th century Perpendicular work.

WORSBROUGH, ST. MARY SE350026

Some Norman work survives in the chancel, including one complete window on the north side. The eastern angle quoins are large irregular blocks, hinting at an earlier date, but the walls are of Norman rather than Overlap thickness 2 ft. 11 ins. (0.88 m.). The chancel arch is a reconstructed Norman piece with unusual ornament. There is later medieval and early 19th century work elsewhere. The monument to Roger Rockley, 1534, is of timber, with effigies of the deceased in life and as a corpse.

Pre-Conquest Sculpture in South Yorkshire

INTRODUCTION

In comparison with some other parts of northern England, South Yorkshire cannot be said to be unduly rich in pre-Conquest and early Romanesque sculpture, but an interesting series of carved stones survive, about two dozen in all, divided between fourteen different churches. There has been some controversy over the dating of several of these stones, some being almost certainly post-Conquest in actual date if not in style. For the purposes of this survey, sculpture will be included which shows, or has been thought to show, pre-Conquest influence. The concept of the Overlap so well seen in the church architecture is again present.

The stones were first brought together in a single account by C. F. Innocent[1] in 1910, being briefly described and a few illustrated with small photographs. A more comprehensive account appeared in the pages of the *Yorkshire Archaeological Journal* five years later[2] when W. G. Collingwood, the great pioneer in the field of pre-Conquest sculpture in the north of England, described and attempted to date all known Saxon sculpture in the West Riding of Yorkshire. He illustrated most pieces by scale drawings. Most of the South Yorkshire stones figured again in Collingwood's *magnum opus* *Northumbrian Crosses of the Pre-Norman Age*[3] which appeared in 1927. Here he revised his earlier dating, most dates being brought forward by a century or so. This change of view, along with Collingwood's concept of an Overlap between Saxon and Norman sculpture, was challenged by Professor Baldwin Brown ten years later in a work[4] in which only a few South Yorkshire pieces receive mention except for what he terms the 'Rotherham Group', the late crosses at Barnburgh, Rawmarsh and Thrybergh, which he illustrates and discusses at length.

Little work has been carried out on the early sculpture of South Yorkshire over the last forty years. At the time of writing a corpus of the Anglo-Saxon sculpture over the whole of the north of England, published by the British Academy under the general editorship of Rosemary Cramp, is under preparation. The volume dealing with the sculpture of the former West Riding is not scheduled to appear for some years.

The stones included in this survey below have all been described in print previously,(although not necessarily illustrated), with the exception of the two early pieces from Darfield which came to light during an inspection of the church by the South Yorkshire Archaeology Service. The technique used to prepare the illustrations has been to make a measured drawing of the stone, corrected with the aid of photographs taken with oblique lighting from different directions. It is quite probable that further examples remain as yet unrecorded, most likely re-used in medieval church fabrics.

In compiling the notes below, and especially those with regard to the dating of the South Yorkshire sculpture, the writer is most grateful for the kind assistance of Mr. J. T. Lang of Durham, a member of the team currently working on the British Academy corpus.

BARNBURGH

A cross shaft of local Magnesian Limestone just under 6 ft. 7 ins. (2.0 m.) in height, 1 ft. 3 ins. (0.38 m.) by 1 ft. 1 in. (0.34 m.), tapering slightly upwards before expanding again just below the head, which has been broken away. Found in the churchyard in two pieces in the 19th century, and re-erected in the church, to the west of the western pillar of the north arcade, early this century. Despite Baldwin Brown's assertion that the whole stone bears a "distinctive Anglo-Saxon stamp"[5] this is really a thoroughly Romanesque piece with only an echo of earlier forms in the three-cord plait with pellets on the lower part of the south face. Both Baldwin Brown's and Collingwood's[6] descriptions of the stone are inaccurate. The acanthus leaves on the west are very much Romanesque, as are the rather crude figures in very high relief, another feature never found in pre-Conquest sculpture but with parallels in some 12th century Irish work such as the cross at Dysert O'Dea (County Clare). The similarities to the figure and acanthus leaves on St. Leonard's Cross at Thrybergh are so apparent that it might be assumed that the two crosses are the work of the same sculptor.

BARNBURGH Cross now in church

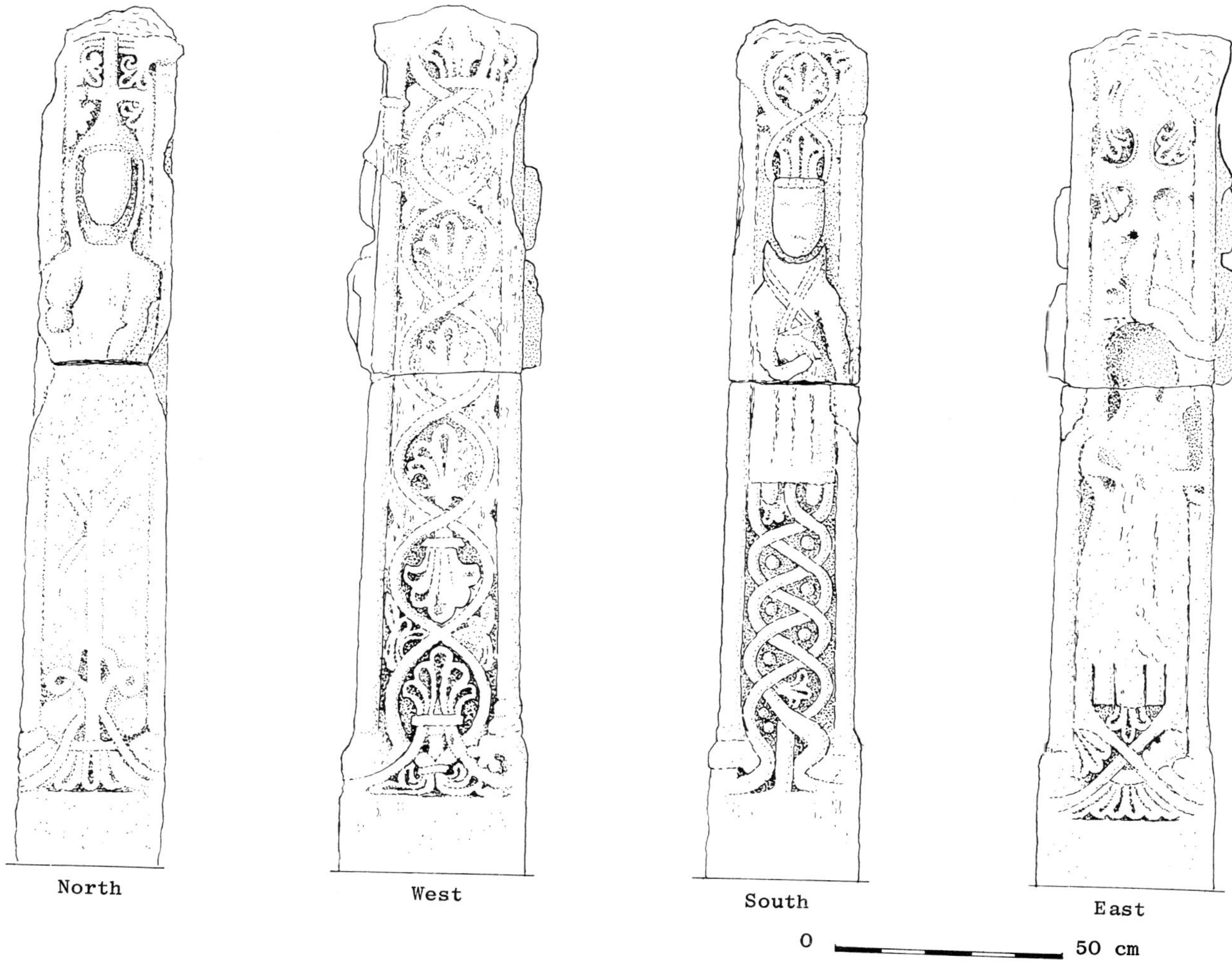

BRADFIELD

A cross fashioned from a single piece of gritstone, 3 ft. 8 ins. (1.12 m.) high, and with a shaft 1 ft. 0 in. (0.3 m.) wide at its base tapering to 10 ins. (0.25 m.) at the neck, the head being 1 ft. 3 ins. (0.37 m.) across the arms. The shaft is rectangular in section with slightly rounded angles, and quite plain. The head, of distinct hammerhead form, has five raised bosses within an enclosing line. This design may be a reflection of a wooden cross bearing a metal appliqué, as may be the rounded angles of the shaft. Both features link with a series of crosses in Staffordshire having circular shafts and dating from after 950. The hammerhead form of the head suggests a later date, perhaps not long before the Norman Conquest.

The cross was found in 1870 at N.G.R. SK263920, not far from the present Cross Inn, and was placed in the parish church in 1883, set against the north wall of the north aisle.

BRADFIELD Cross now in St Nicholas' Church

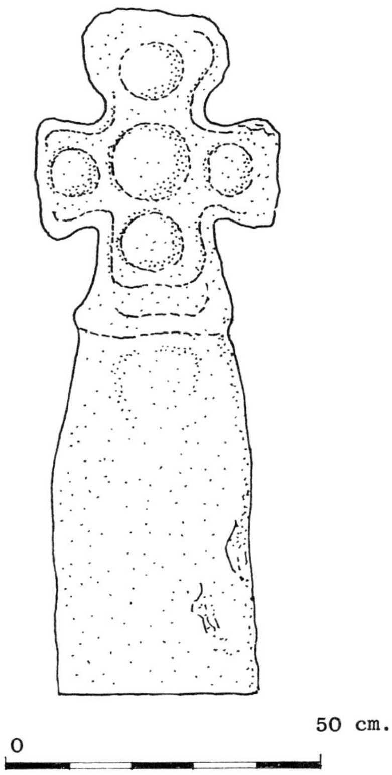

CAWTHORNE

The church at Cawthorne contains no architectural feature of pre-13th century date, yet has a valuable collection of pre-Conquest and Overlap sculpture. This comprises three pieces, two shaft fragments and a head, now reconstructed as part of a free-standing cross in the churchyard to the west of the church, a second cross head built into the external face of the east gable of the north chapel, and a font bowl now in the south aisle.

(i) The lower part of the churchyard cross shaft is formed by a section of ancient shaft 3 ft. 1 in. (0.93 m.) high, and roughly rectangular in plan, c. 1 ft. 3 ins. (0.39 m.) by 11 ins. (0.27 m.), bearing crudely cut and irregularly disposed ornament. What appears to be the principal face, now on the west, bears what appears to be the lower part of a figure, or perhaps two opposed figures, cut in relief. The remainder of the ornament is incised, 'D' motifs, either set in squares or, on the east face, apparently scattered at random, and a badly drawn plait design on the north. The 'D' motifs, seen again at Penistone, and perhaps at Ecclesfield, are evidence of a late date (similar patterns occur on a hogback tombstone at Hexham now thought to be post-Conquest work of the late 11th century) as is the plait.

(ii) The upper, much smaller section of the shaft, set just below the head, is 1 ft. 2 ins. (0.35 m.) high, 9 ins. (0.24 m.) by 7 ins. (0.17 m.) in section at the base tapering asymetrically to 9 ins. (0.23 m.) by 4 ins. (0.11 m.). The asymetry is not the product of later damage; the mason appears to have worked with a misshapen stone from the first, the panel borders following the irregularity which might perhaps be the result of an accident whilst the stone was being cut. Collingwood[7] doubts that the two pieces are sections of the same shaft, and the upper piece does seem too small for the head, yet the upper section bears the same panel borders (doubled on the west) as the lower. Collingwood's illustrations of one face and one edge of this upper section show incised patterns no longer traceable, if they are not simply his conjecture. The only designs now apparent are 'D' motifs at the top of the panel on the south and west, and perhaps a detached 'D' a little further down on the east.

(iii) The cross head is intact, and measures 2 ft. 1 in. (0.63 m.) across the arms, which are of slightly 'hammerhead' form. On the main (west) face a central raised motif, occupying the centre and lower arm, has been cut back, presumably when the stone was re-used as walling material. Its form suggests that it may have been a figure of Christ in Majesty, as seen on a cross from St. Mary's church, Castlegate, in York. The other arms have trapezoidal panels with 'D' motifs. The reverse (east) face is much plainer, with an intact circular boss ringed by a cable moulding in the centre, and a single incised line paralleling the edge of the head, with four small adjacent panels on the lower arm.

(iv) The second cross head, built into the church wall, is larger, measuring 2 ft. 9 ins. (0.85 m.) across the arms. In overall design the exposed face is very similar to the churchyard cross, with a raised figure (again perhaps Christ in Majesty) which has been cut back, although not quite as ruthlessly as on the smaller head. Collingwood's drawing[8] showing leaf scroll ornament on the arms is incorrect (he admits it to be "not quite certain"). Close examination shows the weathered ornament to be patterns based on the 'D' motif.

CAWTHORNE   Cross in churchyard

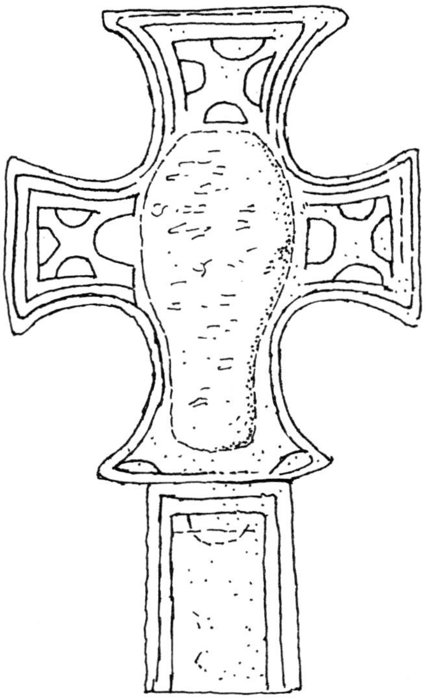

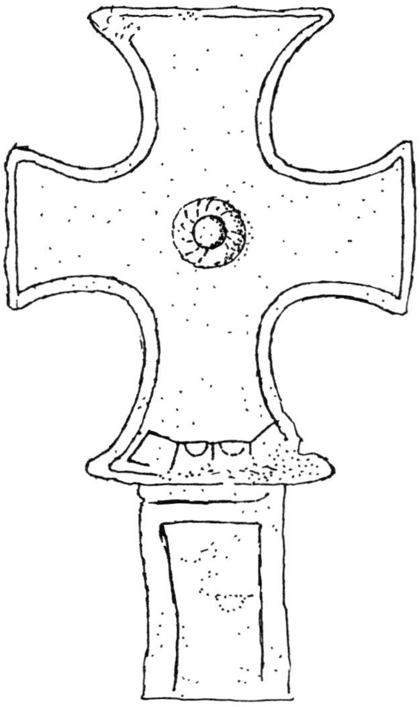

(iii) Head

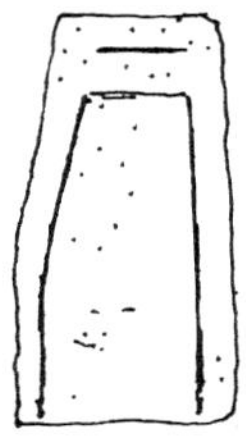

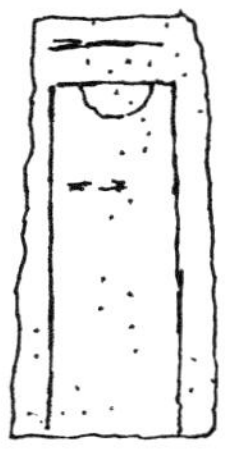

(ii) Upper portion of shaft

West   North   East   South

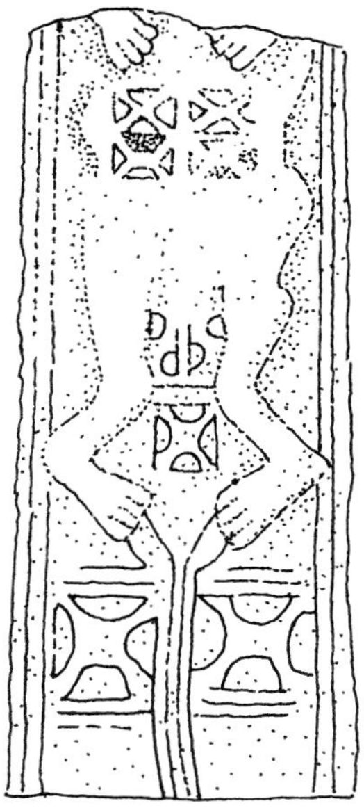

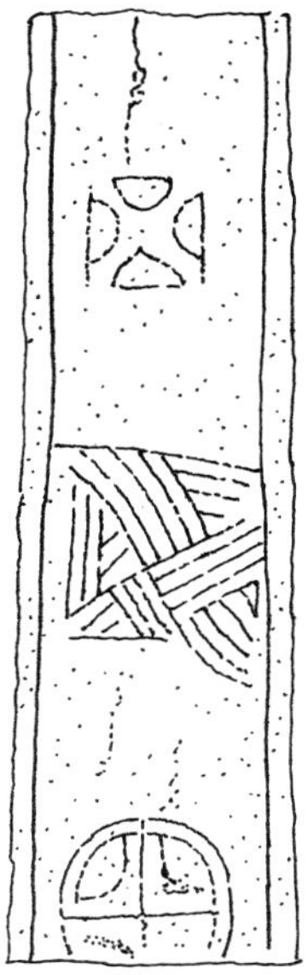

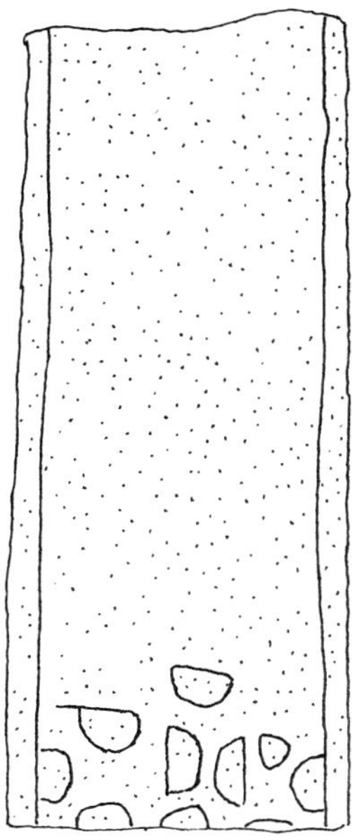

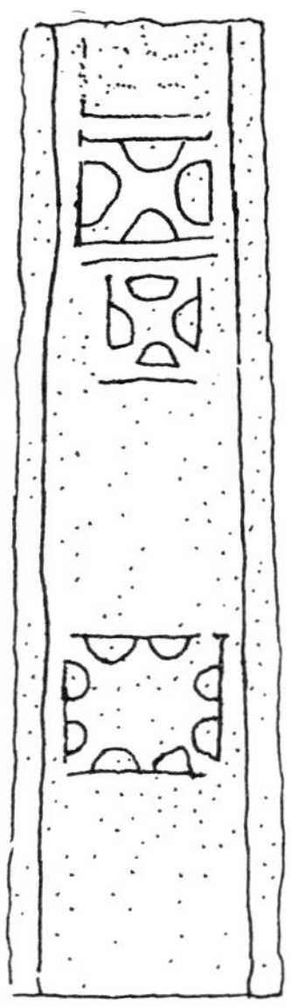

(i) Lower portion of shaft

South face

CAWTHORNE Early font in church (v)

North face

East face

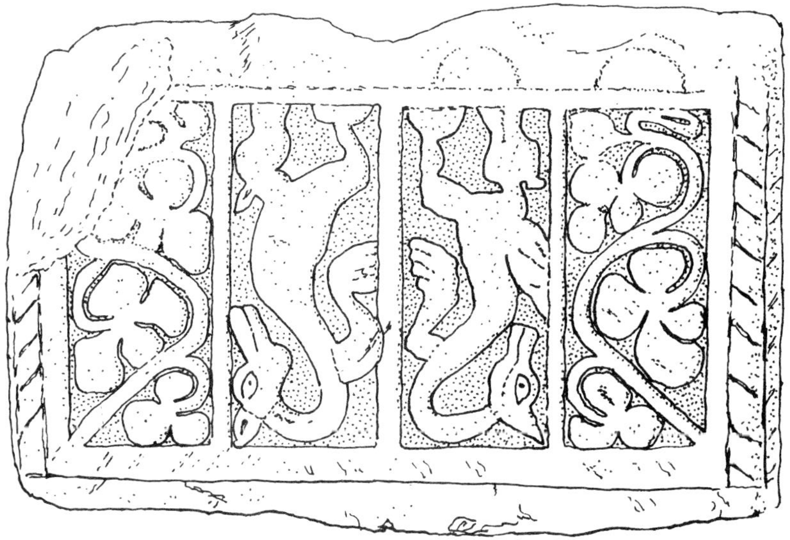

West face

CAWTHORNE Head of cross built into east end of north chapel (iv)

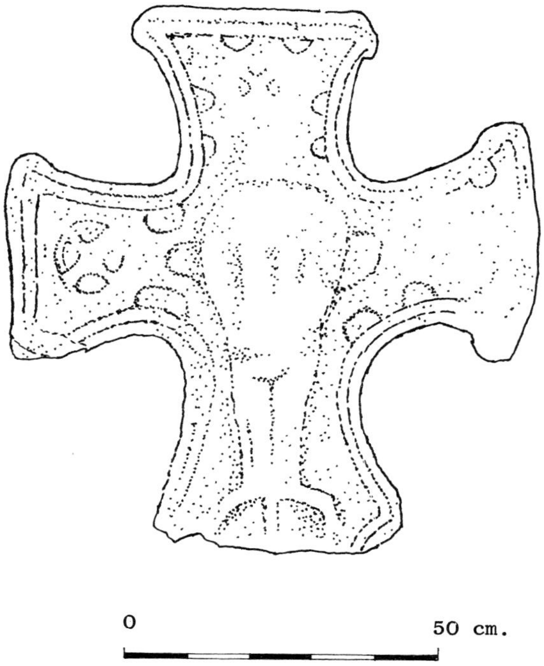

The 'hammerhead' form of both cross heads evidences affinities with a group of crosses in Galloway (south-west Scotland). Other evidence suggests that there was a cultural connection with Yorkshire sites.

(v) The early font, found in the grounds of Cannon Hall some years ago and brought into the church, consists of a trapezoidal, sides of 1 ft. 10 ins. (0.55 m.) to 2 ft. 4 ins. (0.7 m.), grit-stone bowl, with a double cable moulding at each angle and four panels with relief decoration on each face, each headed with a sunken semicircle giving the appearance of an arcade of round-headed arches. The motifs in the panels are a mixture of pre-Conquest and Romanesque. The rather 'zig-zag' vine scroll is of the former (a parallel is seen on a cross shaft at Collingham, near Leeds) and the peculiar little two-headed dragons and cross paté motifs (common on late 11th and early 12th century cross slab grave covers at several localities in South Yorkshire) distinctly of the latter. The bowl is thus a true Overlap piece, and can perhaps be dated to the middle of the 11th century. The font bowl from High Hoyland (now at Skelmanthorpe) is obviously a product of the same school, but perhaps a little later still in date.

CONISBROUGH

A fragment of cross shaft 1 ft. 7 ins. (0.49 m.) and 11 ins. (0.27 m.) by 8 ins. (0.21 m.) in section, now on the floor at the west end of the south aisle of this important pre-Conquest church. The stone is illustrated by Collingwood[9] and reconstructed somewhat optimistically by him as the upper part of the shaft of a wheel-headed cross, which he dated to the late 10th century.
The decoration is of a type classed as Anglo-Scandinavian, including both earlier Anglian forms (the vine scroll) and a Viking-influenced version of interlace with closed circuits rather than a geometrically proper layout. It is probably unwise to be more specific than to suggest an overall 10th century dating.

CONISBROUGH Cross shaft fragment in church

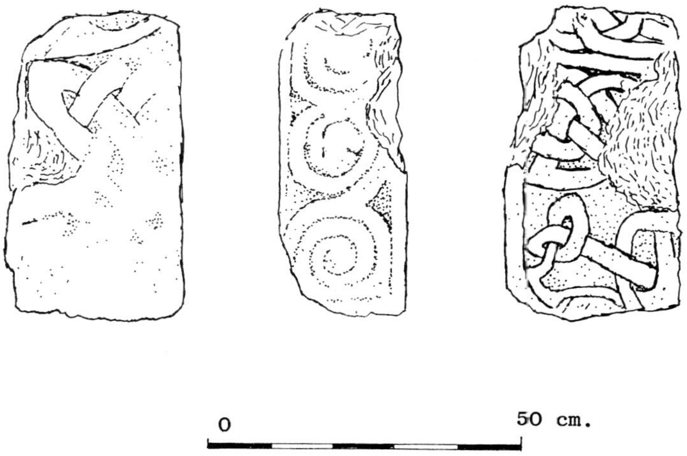

DARFIELD

Two fragments built into the walling of the medieval church are both of relatively early date:

(i) Built into the internal face of the south wall of the tower, c. 11 ft. 6 ins. (3.5 m.) above the present floor level. A stone 1 ft. 2 ins. (0.36 m.) by 6 ins. (0.15 m.) bearing a 'marigold' or petalled rosette flanked by panels of interlace, with on the far left a remnant of a second disc-like motif. The form of the stone suggests that this is not a cross shaft. It may have formed part of a grave slab, or perhaps more likely a closure panel (a series of which would have formed a screen surrounding the sanctuary or altar). The design finds parallels in the earlier work at Hexham and York, and dates the stone to the 8th century.

DARFIELD Pre-Conquest sculptural fragments built into church fabric.

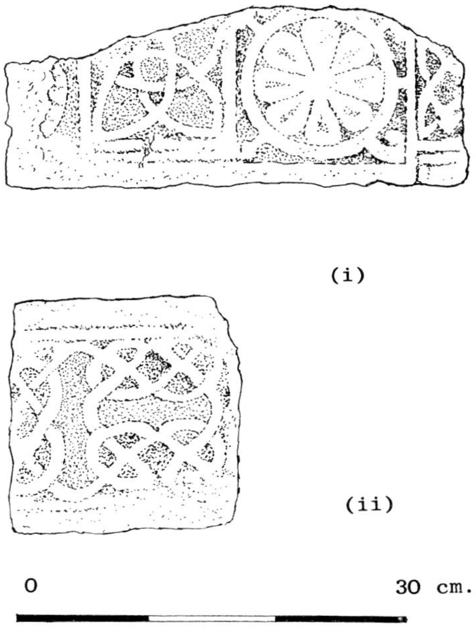

(ii) A fragment 7 ins. (0.17 m.) square now built into the internal face of the south wall of the chapel on the north side of the chancel, just above floor level. Good quality interlace, obviously of pre-Viking date, on what is probably a cross shaft fragment of late 8th or early 9th century origin.

ECCLESFIELD

A cross shaft and base, found in 1892 in the re-laying of a churchyard path near the west door of the church, and now standing in the south transept. The shaft, 4 ft. 10 ins. (1.47 m.) high, is in two pieces now cemented together, 1 ft. 0 in. (0.31 m.) by 9 ins. (0.22 m.) in section at the base and tapering slightly upwards. The base is 4 ft. 9 ins. (1.44 m.) by 2 ft. 0 in. (0.62 m.) in plan, with equal-sized sockets for two shafts only 9 ins. (0.22 m.) apart. The surviving shaft is decorated on one face only. The opposite side and edges have plain panels enclosed by incised lines. The decoration is crude and irregular, consisting of a series of

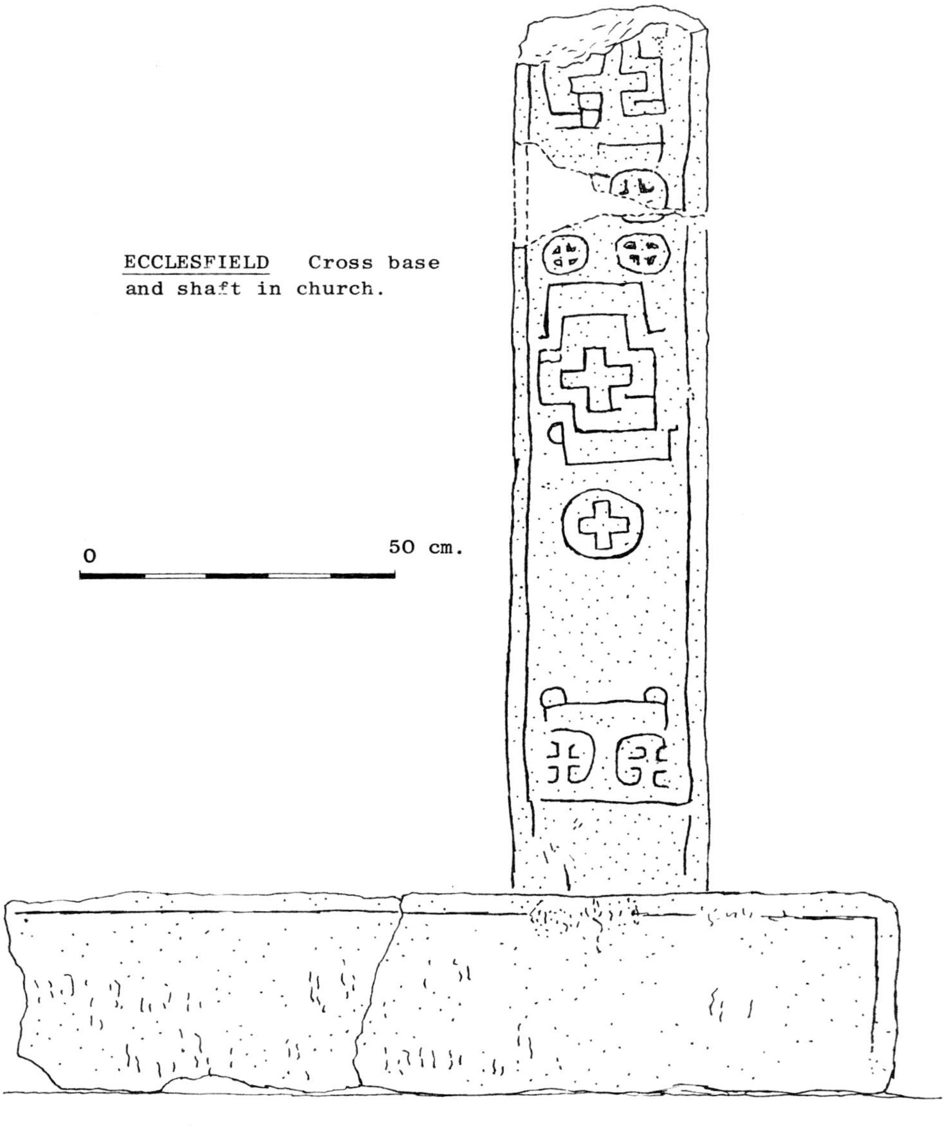

ECCLESFIELD Cross base and shaft in church.

crosses, some within circles, a form reminiscent of those on the late hogback at Hexham, with the 'D' motif appearing once or twice. The base has a simple incised line just short of its edge both on the sides and top surface, producing what Collingwood[10] terms an "Anglo-Saxon moulding". Both base and shaft are cut in local gritstone.

The crude nature of the decoration puts this stone in the same class as the crosses at Cawthorne and Penistone, and it must be ascribed tentatively to the same date, that is to the 11th century. The twin sockets in the base are unusual (although a rough stone with a similar pair of sockets is to be found in the churchyard at Bolsterstone, SK271968). If both sockets were in use at the same time it must be assumed that the crosses were of unequal height, to allow room for their heads.

HIGH HOYLAND

Several fragments of pre-Conquest and medieval sculpture are built into the inner face of the north wall of the nave of this church, a structure rebuilt early this century. The earliest and most interesting piece (i) stood free on a shelf and was stolen from the church, now redundant, in 1979. A 1980 newspaper report[11] of its discovery in the United States seems to have been without foundation.

(i) The missing cross head consisted of the centre and lateral arms of a stone of late 8th or early 9th century date, with a 'marigold' on one face and what was presumably a raised boss (cut back) flanked by vine scroll on the other. The former motif suggests a rather earlier date than the latter, and hints that the vine scroll face might be a secondary re-cutting.

(ii) A fragment, stolen along with (i), which appeared at first sight to be the upper arm of the same cross head but which was considered by Collingwood[12] to be a part of a similar but not identical piece of sculpture, with a plait rather than a vine scroll on the main face.

(iii) What appear to be rather unequal halves of two similar cross heads placed together in the wall, showing almost circular 'armpits', a form with parallels in Galloway. Probably 11th century.

(iv) One arm of a cross head, of an unusual 'battle-axe' shape, again perhaps an 11th century piece.

(v) A fragment of free-style sculpture showing an animal (Agnus Dei?) in relief in a sunk panel. Difficult to date but may perhaps be pre-Conquest.

HIGH HOYLAND Pre-Conquest Sculptural Fragments

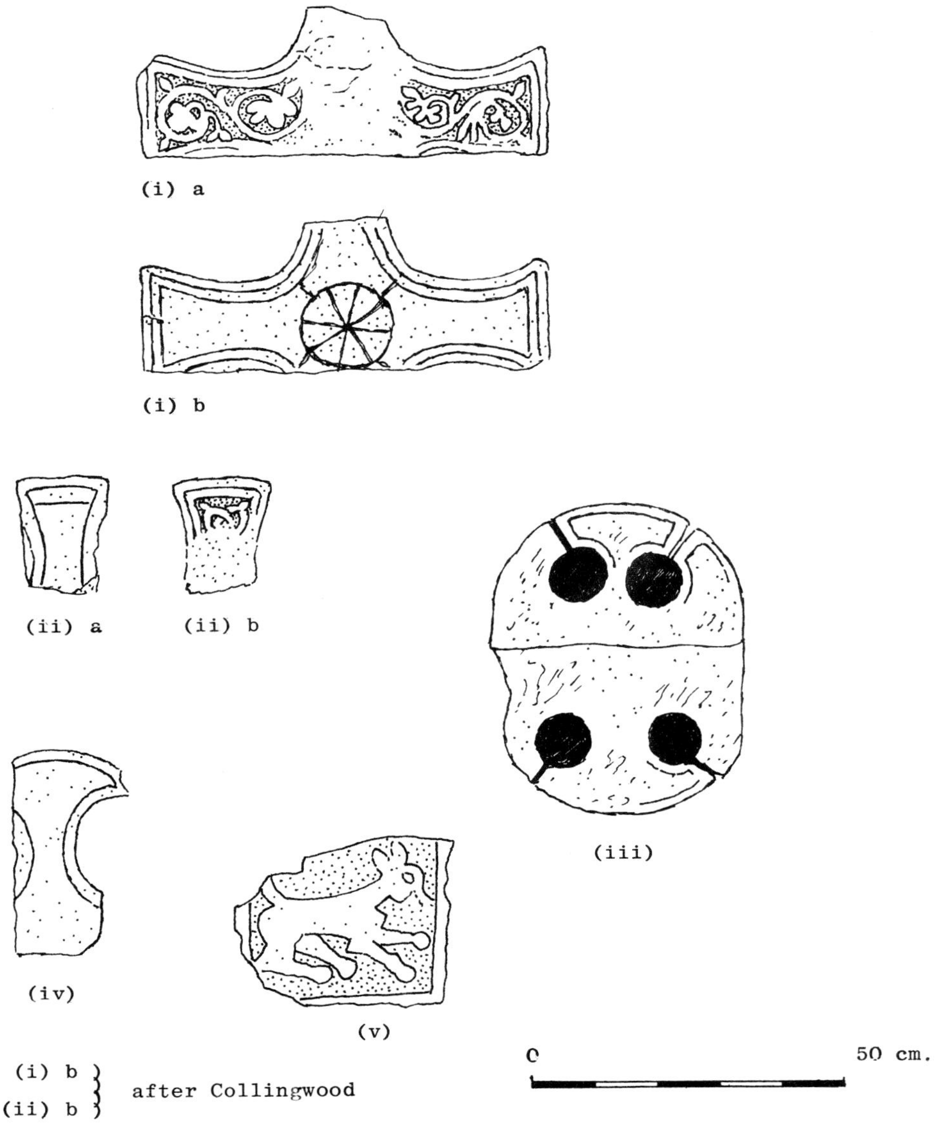

The bowl of the old font from High Hoyland is now in use in the modern church at Skelmanthorpe (SE230104), $2\frac{1}{2}$ miles (4.0 km.) to the west in West Yorkshire. This is an impressive Overlap piece with many similarities to the Cawthorne font; the tree scroll and angular vine scroll motifs are again present. The round-arched heads to the panels here form an intersecting arcade, very much a Norman feature (with parallels at Durham and Lastingham in the 1080s and 1090s), perhaps suggesting that this is a few years later in date than the Cawthorne example, although quite possibly carved by the same hand.

East face

West face

North face

South face

0 50 cm

HIGH HOYLAND Font bowl (now at Skelmanthorpe)

MEXBOROUGH

A substantial section of a sandstone cross shaft, 4 ft. 8 ins. (1.42 m.) long, tapering from 1 ft. 1 in. (0.34 m.) by 9 ins. (0.22 m.) at its base to 1 ft. 0 in. (0.30 m.) by 7 ins. (0.185 m.) at its top. The stone was at one time fixed upright against the chancel wall but for the last forty years has lain on the floor at the east end of the south aisle. The exposed face is mostly occupied by a single rectangular panel (its top missing) with double incised border lines, the outer pair of which curl inwards below the panel base into spirals of alternating indents and small incised circles (Collingwood's drawing[13] is incorrect). Below the spirals is the head of a broader rectangular panel. On the exposed edge of the stone, much worn, only simple incised border lines can be seen. The reverse face, accessible only with difficulty, appears to bear a design identical to the front. The stone lies on one edge which could not be inspected. The simplicity of the designs make this a difficult stone to date, but it probably belongs to the 10th or 11th century.

MEXBOROUGH Cross shaft in church

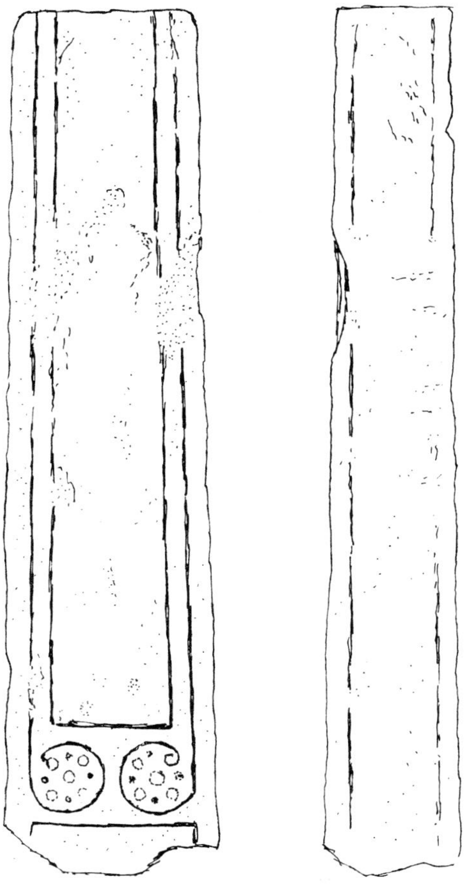

(a) (b)

Side opposite (a) appears to be identical
Edge opposite (b) not seen

0 50 cm.

PENISTONE

A section of a stone which is evidently part of a cross shaft, now forming one of the angle quoins at the north-east corner of the nave, 10 ft. 0 in. (3.1 m.) above the present floor level, and visible from the north aisle, which is continued eastward to form a chapel. The fragment, of local gritstone, is 2 ft. 6 ins. (0.77 m.) long tapering from 1 ft. 3 in. (0.37 m.) to 1 ft. 1 in. (0.34 m.). There are double incised borders, with between them a single square panel subdivided into four smaller squares, each with various configurations of the 'D' motif used in a manner very reminiscent of the Cawthorne cross shaft. Probably of 11th century date.

PENISTONE Cross shaft in church.

RAWMARSH

A cross shaft and base which for many years stood in the churchyard on the south side of the parish church has now been moved into the base of the tower. The shaft, of local sandstone, is 5 ft. 11 ins. (1.81 m.) high, 1 ft. 1 in. (0.34 m.) by 9 ins. (0.24 m.) at the base tapering to 11 ins. (0.29 m.) by 8 ins. (0.21 m.). The stone is very badly weathered. Each angle has a chamfer ornamented by bosses (compare the Thrybergh crosses) which have been eroded almost entirely away, the chamfer being simply stopped 4 ins. (0.11 m.) above the base. The present east face (on the west when the stone stood in the churchyard) has a raised zig-zag line and two small bosses just below the top. North and south edges each have sunken foliage patterns with pellets, that on the south being the better preserved. The west face is now featureless. The irregular base has a peculiar little piece of high-relief carving on the north side of the shaft, apparently depicting foliage but hard to explain.

Despite Baldwin Brown's terming the stone "obviously Saxonic"[14] it has no feature to suggest a date other than in the second half of the 12th century.

The cross head shown in Baldwin Brown's photograph[15] and said by him to be "suspiciously modern" has now disappeared.

RAWMARSH Churchyard cross now in church

South side of head

North side of head

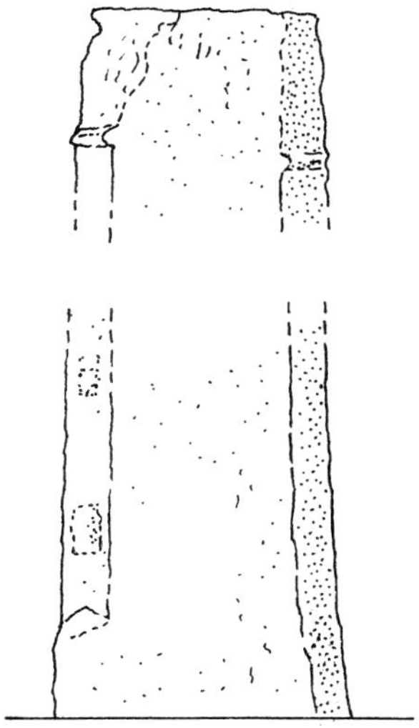

West face

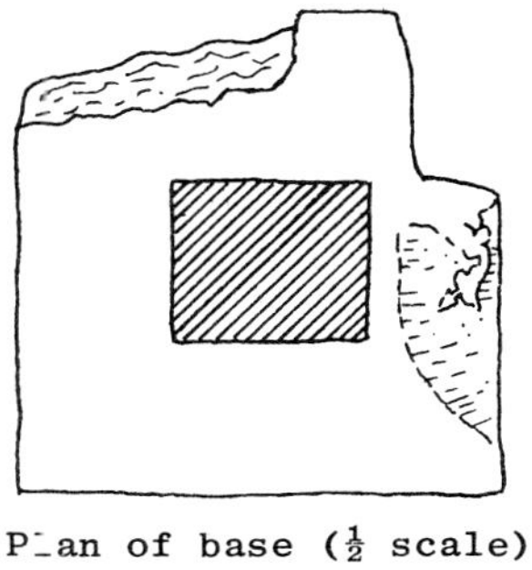

Plan of base (½ scale)

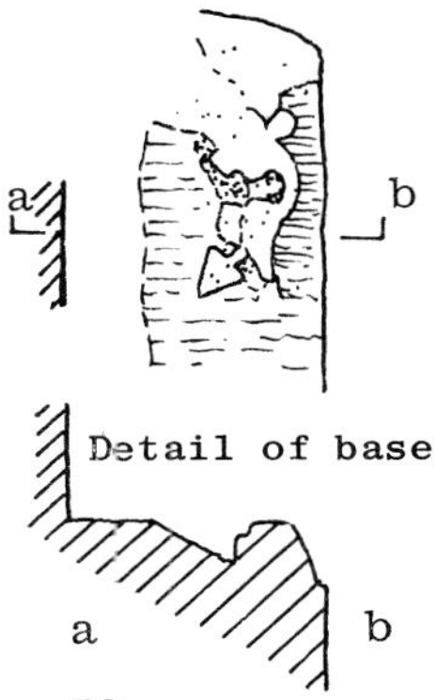

Detail of base

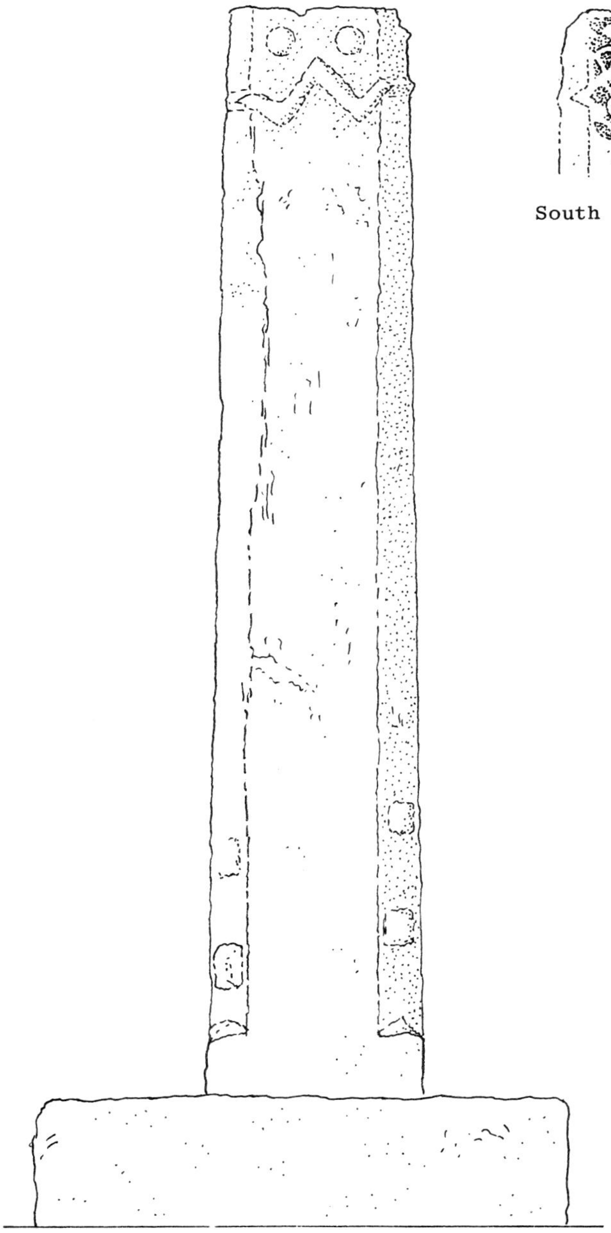

East face

SHEFFIELD

A large piece of a fine cross shaft of sandstone, 4 ft. 9 ins. (1.45 m.) tall and 1 ft. 9 ins. (0.33 m.) at its base, tapering to 1 ft. 4 ins. (0.40 m.) by 11 ins. (0.29 m.). The original stone is now in the British Museum, but a cast is displayed in Sheffield City Museum.

SHEFFIELD Cross shaft now in British Museum

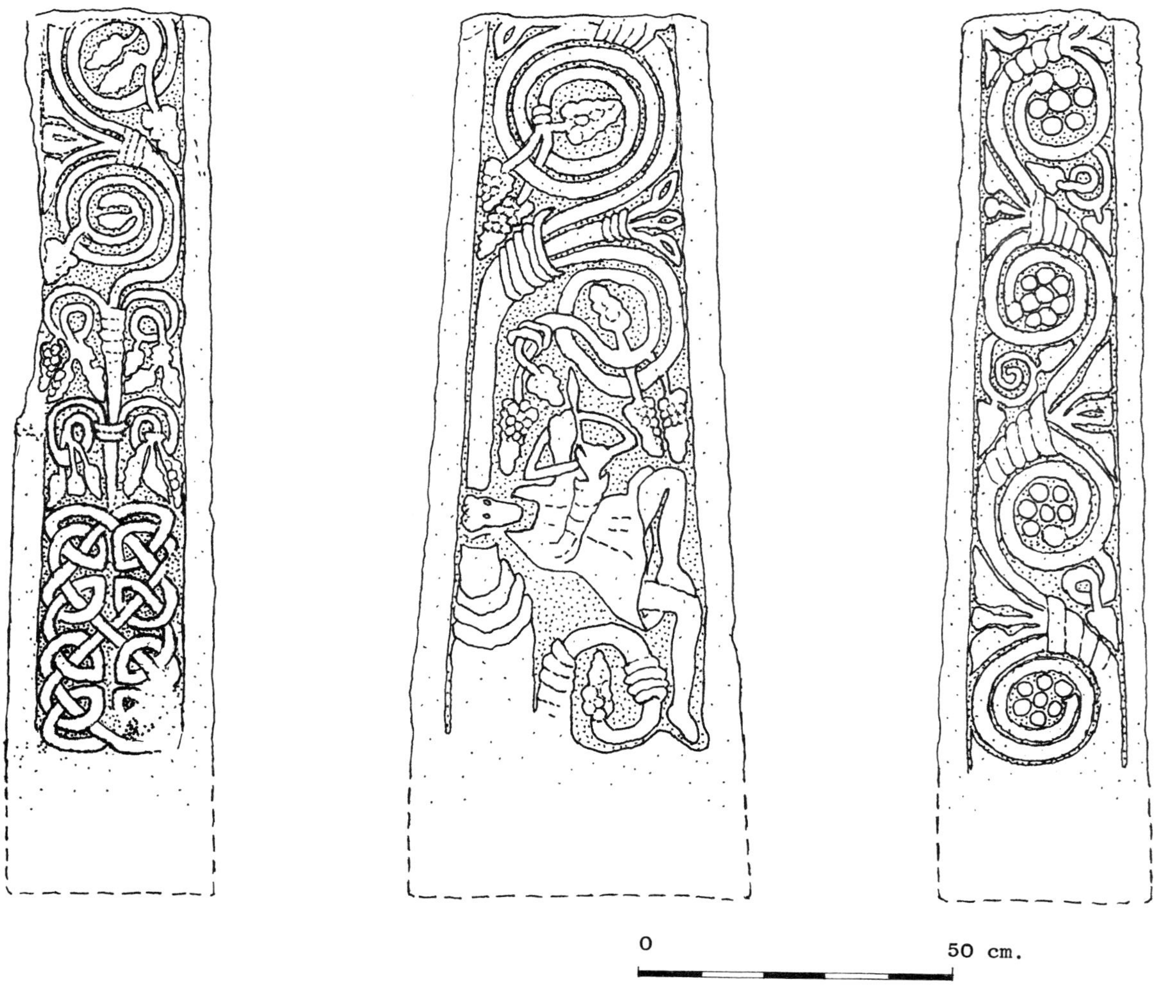

The cross shaft is generally thought to have been discovered early in the 19th century by a Mr. William Staniforth, whilst it was doing duty as a hardening trough in a cutler's workshop in Sheffield Park, being brought to his garden in Whitham Road, Sheffield, and later moved to a garden in Oakholme Road before being presented to the British Museum[17]. Howarth[18] suggests that the shaft may be a part of the Sheffield churchyard cross known to have been pulled down in 1570. Some doubt is cast on the story of the discovery of the cross by Collingwood[19] who states that C. F. Innocent, the Sheffield architect and antiquary, believed that the stone might have been brought into Sheffield from Derbyshire by a 19th century owner.

One face of the shaft has been destroyed when the stone was hollowed out to make a trough. The other face bears an archer shooting up into a vine scroll which Collingwood describes as "thick and stiff", characteristics which he rather exaggerates in his drawing. The identification of the archer figures on several Saxon crosses, including Ruthwell, St. Andrew Auckland, Bakewell and Bradbourne, has recently been discussed by Farrell[20] who considers the recurrent motif (if not an importation from secular mythology) to be symbolic of the attacks of evil. The sides of the shaft bear vine scroll and a plait pattern. Collingwood's original dating of this stone as late Anglian work, that is before any Viking influence in sculpture, of c. 850[21] is perhaps more acceptable than his later[22] ascription of the piece to the 10th century. The stone is certainly a member of the 'Derbyshire Group' of crosses, the similarities of the vine scroll on its surviving face to that on the east side of the churchyard cross at Eyam being very striking, sufficient to make it quite likely that they were the work of the same hand.

SPROTBOROUGH

A small section of what is probably a cross shaft, built into the east face of a buttress on the south side of the chancel, just above ground level. The exposed side of the stone is only 1 ft. 2 ins. (0.36 m.) long, tapering from 7 ins. (0.17m.) to 6½ ins. (0.16 m.) A short section of incised scroll-like ornament is visible, which Collingwood[23] classes as "debased", although in fact it appears to be quite a carefully controlled piece of work markedly different from the crude and late forms at Cawthorne and Ecclesfield. The stone might be as early as the late 8th or early 9th century. If it was removed from the wall, a closer dating might be possible from the ornament on its other faces.

SPROTBROUGH Fragment of cross shaft

THRYBERGH

Two cross shafts remain at Thrybergh, both still in the open air and unprotected:

(i) ST. LEONARD'S CROSS

Some years ago this stood at the east end of the village, within a small cemetery, but it has since been brought to the churchyard where it is now sited on the south side of the path just inside the entrance gate. The shaft, set on a plain rectangular base, is 4 ft. 4 ins. (1.31 m.) high and 1 ft. 1 in. (0.33 m.) by 9 ins. (0.24 m.) at the base, without any perceptible taper. The stone is white Magnesian Limestone, and must have been imported from quarries at least 1¼ miles (2.0 km.) to the east. The north face bears a ring-twist with pellets, a somewhat 'opened out' version of a motif common in 10th century Anglo-Scandinavian sculpture, but with the "giveaway" of a single acanthus leaf at the base, very much in the style of the solitary trefoil which appears in the otherwise archaic three-cord plait on the Barnburgh cross. The west face has free-style motifs crudely carved in relief, at the foot a figure holding a book beneath a pointed arch, with above an animal (Agnus Dei?) and the feet of a figure (a Crucifixion?) at the top. Below the animal are acanthus leaves which appear again in an irregular scroll, much weathered, on the south. The east face has chamfered edges with irregularly placed bosses, coinciding with more acanthus leaves which spring from either side of a cross shaft, the shaft rising from a triangular mount.

(ii) THE VILLAGE GREEN CROSS

The second Thrybergh cross now stands incongruously on the pavement among a small group of modern houses beyond the main road east of the church, but apparently once stood on a vanished village green[24]. The shaft is 3 ft. 8 ins. (1.11 m.) high and 1 ft. 2 ins. (0.36 m.) by 10 ins. (0.25 m.) at the top, cut in dark local gritstone. The angles are chamfered with regularly spaced bosses, and the edges completely plain. The west face bears a cross shaft flanked by acanthus-like leaves, and the east face a simple incised sword set below an arcuate line of indents which is presumably part of the head design. The sinkings for four pegs which held the head in position remain. The stone has no pre-Conquest affinities (both cross shaft and sword would not be out of place on a 12th or 13th century cross slab grave cover) but is included for its similarities to the later motifs on St. Leonard's Cross.

Collingwood[25] dates both crosses to the late 12th or early 13th century. Some authorities have questioned whether St. Leonard's Cross might not in fact be an earlier stone partly re-cut, but in view of its affinities with Barnburgh this seems unlikely. It is probably safest to look upon its ring-twist as a strangely late appearance of a pre-Conquest motif on what is otherwise a distinctly medieval piece of carving, the product of a sculptor whose forte seems to have been foliage patterns and the occasional use of archaic motifs rather than relief figure sculpture.

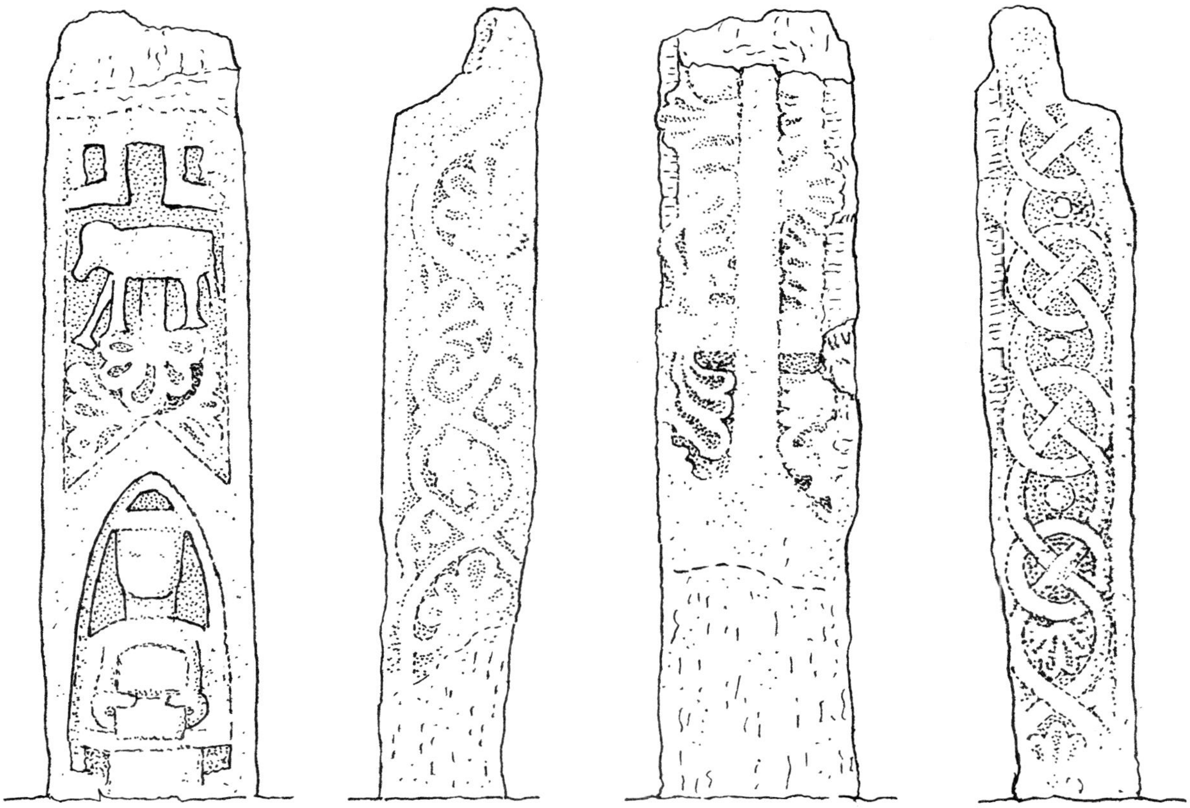

West Face | South Side | East Face | North Side

THRYBERGH Cross I (St Leonard's Cross)

Cross II (The "Village Green" Cross)

0 50 cm.

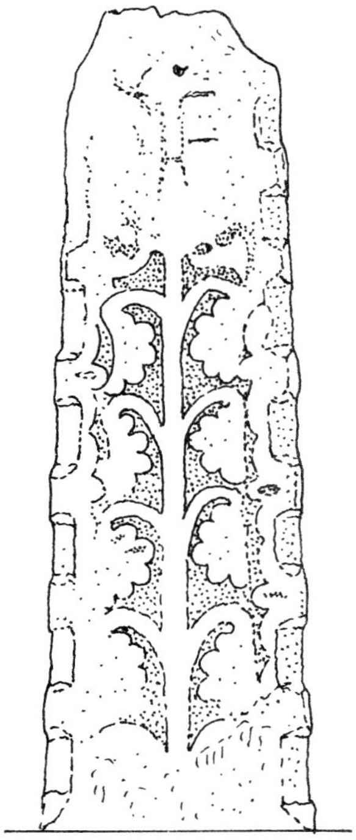

West Face

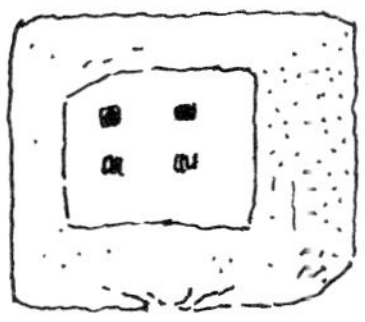

Top of Shaft

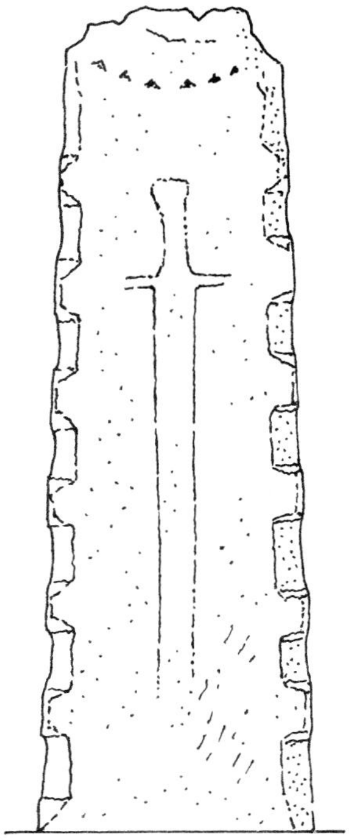

East Face

REFERENCES

1. Innocent, C. F. — Early Christian Remains in the District, *British Association Handbook and Guide to Sheffield.* 88-95, 1910

2. Collingwood, W. G. — Anglian and Anglo-Danish Sculpture in the West Riding of Yorkshire, *Yorkshire Archaeological Journal* XXIII, 129-254, 1915

3. Collingwood, W. G. — *Northumbrian Crosses of the Pre-Norman Age,* London: Faber & Gwyer 1927

4. Brown, Baldwin G. — Anglo-Saxon Sculpture, *The Arts in Early England* VI pt. II, 1937

5. Ibid. — 147

6. Collingwood 1915 — 135

7. Bailey, R. N. — *Viking Age Sculpture,* 148-149. Collins, 1980

8. Collingwood 1915 — 152

9. Ibid. — 153

10. Collingwood 1927 — Op. cit. 107

11. Collingwood 1915 — Op. cit. 172

12. Yorkshire Post — Yorkshire Post 4-1-80, p.1

13. Collingwood 1915 — Op. cit. 185

14. Ibid. — 219

15. Brown — Op. cit. 147

16. Ibid. — Plate XXXIX No. 2

17. Information from Miss P. Beswick, Sheffield City Museum

18. Howarth, E. — 'The Sheffield Cross', *The Reliquary and Illustrated Archaeologist* July 1907

19. Collingwood 1927 — Op. cit. 75

20. Farrell, R. T. (ed.) — 'The Archer and Associated Figures on the Ruthwell Cross - a Reconsideration'. *Bede and Anglo-Saxon England,* British Archaeological Report 46, 96-117, 1978

21. Collingwood 1915 — Op. cit. 239

22. Collingwood 1927 — Op. cit. 75

23. Collingwood 1915 — Op. cit. 240

24. Armitage, E. S. — *A Key to English Antiquities,* 203. Sheffield: William Townsend 1897

25. Collingwood 1915 — Op. cit. 250

Summary and Conclusions

There are only four 'recognised' pre-Conquest churches in South Yorkshire, yet these four include three quite distinct types. This suggests what is known from other sources, that the area was very much a boundary zone under the influence of different centres, north and south, at different times in history. The same pattern is manifest again a few centuries later when the late medieval timber-framed buildings of the county are studied, a mixture of 'northern' (or Highland) and 'southern' (or Lowland) carpentry types being found.

Of the four 'recognised' Saxon fabrics, St. Peter's church at Conisbrough is without doubt the earliest, showing many similarities to the Northumbrian group of churches of 8th century date. Laughton and Bolton-on-Dearne with their long-and-short quoins are representative of a less well-defined, more southerly tradition, and probably of late 10th century or early 11th century date. With the exception of the isolated Whittingham in Northumberland, Bolton-on-Dearne is one of the northernmost examples of this distinctive quoin type so far recorded, and its short nave is quite different in proportions from that at Conisbrough. The pre-Conquest fabric at Laughton raises many problems, but if indeed the present west tower encases an early crossing of the type greater in width than any of the adjacent arms then a parallel can be found at Stow in Lincolnshire, 25 miles (40 km.) to the east.

Burghwallis is a different type again, heavy and irregular side-alternate quoins being used along herringbone work, a masonry type which, after much controversy, is now agreed to have been in use both before and after the Conquest. The angle quoins, unless they have been re-used, and the form of the south door would argue for a Saxon date here, and the church is probably one of the earliest members of quite a large Yorkshire group using herringbone, of which Kippax (West Yorkshire) is a fine example.

The other three churches studied in detail in this monograph belong to the Overlap category of buildings showing both Saxon and Norman features and probably erected mostly in the second half of the 11th century. Maltby preserves an Overlap tower of not unusual form, with herringbone fabric and small round-headed windows cut straight through the rubble walling, but the remainder of the church was swept away by the Victorians.

Brodsworth and Hooton Pagnell, two buildings which in their original form were probably very similar, are also probably of 11th century date but of a less common and quite distinctive type. Hooton Pagnell, the better preserved of the two, has a relatively short nave, a broad western tower and a small box-like chancel (extended in the 13th century). The relationship of the tower and nave is interesting, the outer faces of the north and south walls of nave and tower being flush without any structural divide, the tower walls being thickened internally. This layout echoes the earlier Skipwith in North Yorkshire[1], but there both tower and nave walls are more characteristically Anglo-Saxon in thickness, 2 ft. 11 ins. (0.88 m.) and 2 ft. 9 ins. (0.85 m.) as compared to 3 ft. 11 ins. (1.2 m.) and 3 ft. 7 ins. (1.1 m.) at Hooton Pagnell. The early work in the tower extends only to the height of the first stage, and the upper parts, sitting rather uncomfortably on the broad base, are 14th century work. Of the surviving architectural features the south door is plain Norman work and the tower arch has been interfered with, but the fine chancel arch, relatively tall and wide, is more reminiscent of Saxon parallels than local Norman work. The slightly 'horseshoe' shape of the arch, its almost bulbous roll moulding and the quite un-Norman form of the capitals and bases of the jamb shafts all point to pre-Conquest influence if not actual date.

At Brodsworth remains survive of a tower and nave of similar plan to those at Hooton Pagnell, but much more mutilated both by later medieval and 19th century alterations. The area of original tower was thrown into the nave c. 1200 when the present tower was built further west, but its north and west walls survive with one or two interesting features. The readiness with which the original tower was removed might be explained by its upper parts having been of timber, which might need replacement after a century or so.

This 11th century church type with an unusually broad western tower carrying a timber superstructure may have had other local representatives. At Darfield the lower stage of the quite massive west tower is of early Norman or Overlap construction. The building history of the remainder of the fabric here is complex and warrants careful study. An engraving of St. Mary's church at Rawmarsh, completely rebuilt in 1839, shows a building with a tall but fairly short nave, a massive western tower the same width as the nave, but with a 15th or 16th century belfry stage rather reminiscent of Bolton-on-Dearne, and a relatively low and narrow chancel which appeared to have been extended eastwards in the 13th or 14th century. Admittedly no example of an early medieval timber belfry stage survives in Yorkshire, but after eight centuries this could hardly be expected. A precedent for a square stone lower stage of greater dimensions than the conventional all-stone tower of the period, and carrying a wooden tower or steeple, can be found a century or so earlier in the Stow-type crossings of a number of the larger Anglo-Saxon churches. Contemporary accounts and illustrations suggest that the towers these carried were made up of a series of receding stages separated by sloping roofs.

It is quite apparent that a number of other pre-Conquest architectural traits survived the Norman Conquest by a century or more in South Yorkshire. Herringbone fabric, although admittedly used on a less lavish scale than at Burghwallis, is seen also at Brodsworth, Campsall, Hooton Pagnell, Kirk Sandall, Maltby, Marr, Owston, Penistone and Thrybergh. In some of these cases other features, for example the fragmentary remains of a fairly massive quoin at Campsall and the unusual dimensions of the nave at Penistone, hint that genuine pre-Conquest fabric survives, but others are almost undoubtedly Norman. At Kirk Sandall the west gable of the originally aisleless nave, only 2 ft. 7 ins. (0.78 m.) thick and with several herringbone courses, has been claimed as of Saxon date, but the south aisle added in the 12th century shows virtually identical rubble fabric and well-squared side-alternate quoins of no great size, suggesting that it must be near contemporary with the original fabric.

Several South Yorkshire churches preserve remains of angle quoins which suggest a pre-Conquest date, but not of a sufficiently distinctive form to be conclusive evidence. The north west quoin of the nave at High Melton is difficult to classify but includes some unusually tall stones which make it look like a crude attempt at long-and-short work. Taken with the unusual dimensions of the nave, short but tall in a manner reminiscent of Bolton-on-Dearne, and the relatively thin 2 ft. 6 ins. (0.75 m.) walls, the nave can be tentatively dated to the 10th or 11th century. Remains of one original angle quoin only at Throapham and Wath on Dearne, coupled with the 2 ft. 2 ins. (0.65 m.) thick nave walls of the former, each of fairly large blocks placed in side-alternate fashion, point a little less conclusively to Overlap or earlier fabric.

Whilst fabric types and angle quoins, coupled with wall thickness and the proportions of individual parts of the building, are the most usual evidences of 11th century or earlier fabric to survive, a few churches retain solitary architectural features which show pre-Conquest influence. Such is the puzzling south door at Finningley with its stripwork surround, set in a church which otherwise seems thoroughly Norman. Perhaps the door is the result of a local mason schooled in the old traditions being employed during the construction of a church at the end of the 11th century or just conceivably it may be an earlier piece re-used and partly remodelled. Turning from the buildings themselves to the sculptural remains, the same picture of an Overlap in traditions or at any rate a survival of archaisms emerges, demonstrated by the four crosses which Baldwin Brown[2] terms the 'Rotherham Group'. He describes the momuments and goes on to say "one might imagine that in this particular district of Yorkshire Saxon carvers had fallen into a Rip van Winkle slumber soon after the epoch of the Conquest, and when they woke up at the time when Romanesque was passing into Gothic, they took up some of the details and motives which they found coming into vogue, and worked them into the general scheme of their monuments which had remained all along inflexibly Saxon".

Perhaps Baldwin Brown exaggerated his point a little and his concept of what was "inflexibly Saxon" needs revision in the light of present knowledge, but the admixture of old and new traditions on St. Leonard's Cross at Thrybergh and the Barnburgh Cross is clear enough. The "slumber" of his masons is difficult to explain bearing in mind the inflow and outflow of regional traditions already seen in the architecture of the area. The Don valley was hardly somnolent in the political sense either, being at one time a major frontier, and in the 12th century the hinterland of the new Norman stronghold at Conisbrough.

Evidence for the continuation, albeit degenerate, of earlier traditions is perhaps easier to accept at a slightly earlier date in the 'Cawthorne' school of cross sculpture, in whose crude and irregular ornament Collingwood[3] saw an indication of "the end of the Anglo-Saxon art movement rather than its beginning". Cawthorne, on the edge of the Pennine moors, fits into the idea of a cultural backwater rather more happily. Coming forward two or three centuries, local vernacular masoncraft is evident both here and at High Hoyland on cross slab grave covers which bear what is evidently a local carver's rendering of 'mainstream' cross designs. The Penistone and probably the Ecclesfield crosses can be classed with the Cawthorne examples as 'debased' late Saxon work. That good quality sculpture was present in the area at an earlier date is, or was, evidenced by a late 8th or early 9th century cross head, recently stolen from High Hoyland church, bearing a classic Anglian vine scroll on one face and a 'marigold' or petalled rosette on the other.

The 'marigold' is seen again on the tantalising Darfield fragment, probably the earliest piece of Christian sculpture so far recorded in the county. The only other piece to merit special attention is the Sheffield cross shaft, whose affinities lie with the Peak District and the 'Bakewell' school in the 9th century.

Returning to the concept of the Saxon-Norman Overlap, the one factor which might explain the relatively numerous examples of this hybrid stile in both the architecture and the sculpture of South Yorkshire is the distance of the area from a major ecclesiastical centre. Such centres, whether cathedral cities such as York and Lincoln, or major monastic houses, exerted an obvious influence on the church buildings and sculpture of the neighbourhood. Here imported ideas took root and spread to the surrounding countryside, but the process took time. South Yorkshire had no such centre in the early Norman period, York, Lincoln and Southwell being almost equally distant. The two major monastic houses, Roche and Monk Bretton, were not founded until the middle of the 12th century, and the Saxon minster church of Conisbrough, despite its situation so close to the Norman castle of the Warennes, was not enlarged and remodelled until the last quarter of the 12th century.

It was probably this absence of Norman influence in the fields of art and architecture (not in politics), that allowed the region its gradual cultural transition, and explains the persistence of some pre-Conquest traditions to the end of the Norman period. This persistence is exemplified structurally by such features as the belfry openings at Burghwallis, and sculpturally by the 11th century font bowl at Cawthorne and St. Leonard's Cross at Thrybergh, which may even be as late as the beginning of the 13th century.

REFERENCES

1. Taylor, H. M. and Taylor, J. — *Anglo-Saxon Architecture*, II, 550-554 Cambridge University Press, 1965
2. Brown, Baldwin G. — Anglo-Saxon Sculpture, *The Arts in Early England* VI pt. II, 142-149, London, John Murray, 1937
3. Collingwood, W. G. — Anglian and Anglo-Danish Sculpture in the West Riding of Yorkshire, *Yorkshire Archaeological Journal*, XXIII, 155, 1915

Plate I

Vertical Archaeology

(1)

(2)

(1) The south wall of the chancel at Laughton-en-le-Morthen.

The red sandstone blocks in the lower part of the wall may either be pre-Conquest work *in situ* or material re-used in a Norman rebuilding. The pilaster buttresses, blocked window and blocked door (to the left of the central buttress) date from this phase. The large windows and diagonal buttress (on the right) are from a second remodelling of the church late in the 14th century. The present priest's door is Victorian.

(2) The north-east quoin of the original pre-Conquest or Overlap nave at Penistone. One of the heavy quoins is a re-used piece of an 11th century cross-shaft, perhaps, like the medieval corbel below, a later repair. To the right of the corbel a small patch of herringbone coursing survives *in situ*.

Plate II

St. Andrew's church, Bolton on Dearne

(1) General south-east view, showing the tall Saxon nave and the longer and lower medieval chancel

(2) The west end of the north aisle, showing the original long and short angle quoin of the Saxon nave

(3) The Saxon window in the south wall of the nave, its outer opening cut through a single massive block of sandstone

Plate III

St. Michael's church, Brodsworth

(1) The west tower from the south, a late 12th or early 13th century addition heightened later in the medieval period

(2) The nave looking east, showing the 15th century chancel arch set within the jambs of its Norman predecessor

(3) The western arch of the north arcade, cut through the north wall of the 11th century tower. On the right of the arch the patched-over toothing of the east wall of the early tower is visible

(4) Unusual medieval carving in the spandrel of the east belfry opening

Plate IV

St. Helen's church, Burghwallis

(1) General south view, showing the herringbone coursing in the nave and chancel

(2) The south door within the rib-vaulted medieval porch. The door appears to be a pre-Conquest feature, with a lower head inserted in the medieval period

(3) Belfry openings on the north side of the tower, with an oculus window below, perhaps originally in the east end, re-set here in the 19th century

Plate V

St. Peter's church, Conisbrough

(1) General south-east view. The exterior gives little evidence of the extensive remains of the Saxon minster church surviving in the present building

(2) Interior looking east. The nave walls may be of 8th century date. Part of an early opening can be seen above the central arch of the 12th century north arcade

Plate VI

All Saints' church, Hooton Pagnell

(1) General south view. Note the broad west tower and angle quoins of the original short chancel, extended in the late 12th or early 13th century. Compare this view with the engraving of the demolished St. Mary's church at Rawmarsh (Plate X)

(2) Interior looking east. The proportions and some details of the fine chancel arch are more Saxon than Norman. The east end lancets are Victorian, but the north arcade is genuine Transitional work of c. 1175 - 1200

Plate VII

All Saints' church, Laughton-en-le-Morthen

(1) General south-east view showing the splendid 14th century tower and spire

(2) A capital of the north arcade, a late 14th century reworking of a 12th century original

(3) At the west end of the north wall of the north aisle, and flanked by late 14th century buttresses, the north wall of a Saxon porticus survives with an impressive original doorway reduced in size in the medieval period

Plate VIII

St. Bartholomew's church, Maltby

(1) The pre-Conquest or Overlap west tower, seen from the south-west. The belfry openings are 15th century remodellings of twin-light originals. The parapet and stone spire are also late medieval work

(2) The interior of the south wall of the tower showing two original round-headed openings, now blocked up

Plate IX

The Problem of the Overlap. Features difficult to date

(1) St. Leonard's Cross, now standing in the churchyard at Thrybergh

(2) The north wall of the nave at Thrybergh, showing the rubble masonry of a short Overlap nave with an ashlar-built western extension of 12th century date, retaining its Norman door

(3) The mysterious re-used frieze at Bolton on Dearne, now built into the internal face of the walls of the ringing chamber in the west tower. It is difficult to find parallels either before or after the Norman Conquest

Plate X

Overlap churches

(1)

(2)

(1) St. Mary's church at Rawmarsh, demolished in in 1831. From this engraving the old church appears to have been an interesting building akin to Hooton Pagnell and Brodsworth, with a tall nave and broad west tower, its upper part perhaps a 15th century replacement of an original timber belfry. The east end of the low chancel (note its string course) looks like an extension of a short square original

(2) The church of St. Peter and St. Paul, Todwick. The north door, a pre-Conquest or Overlap feature reconstructed in the medieval period. The west jamb and west side of the arch (note the rebated voussoirs, also seen at Laughton-en-le-Morthen) are *in situ* 11th century work